MAKING SENSE OF COACHING

D1145793

MAKING SENSE OF
COACHING

ANGÉLIQUE DU TOIT

⑤SAGE

Los Angeles | London | New Delhi
Singapore | Washington DC

Los Angeles | London | New Delhi
Sin gapore | Washington DC

SAGE Publications Ltd
1 Oliver's Yard
55 City Road
London EC1Y 1SP

SAGE Publications Inc.
2455 Teller Road
Thousand Oaks, California 91320

SAGE Publications India Pvt Ltd
B 1/I 1 Mohan Cooperative Industrial Area
Mathura Road
New Delhi 110 044

SAGE Publications Asia-Pacific Pte Ltd
3 Church Street
#10-04 Samsung Hub
Singapore 049483

© Angélique du Toit 2014

First published 2014

Editor: Kirsty Smy
Editorial assistant: Nina Smith
Production editor: Sarah Cooke
Copyeditor: Elaine Leek
Proofreader: Lynda Watson
Marketing manager: Alison Borg
Cover design: Lisa Harper
Typeset by: C&M Digitals (P) Ltd, Chennai, India
Printed in Great Britain by Henry Ling Limited at
The Dorset Press, Dorchester, DT1 1HD

Library of Congress Control Number: 2013940771

British Library Cataloguing in Publication data

A catalogue record for this book is available from
the British Library

MIX
Paper from
responsible sources
FSC
www.fsc.org   FSC™ C013985

ISBN 9780857025609
ISBN 9780857025616 (pbk)

CONTENTS

ABOUT THE AUTHOR

Dr Angélique du Toit is an academic practitioner whose career combines academia as well as experience as an international manager. Angélique has also been an international executive coach for 16 years, supporting the leadership capacity and development of executives in both public and private organizations. She is on the preferred suppliers list as an Executive Coach for a number of organizations in the private sector as well as the NHS register for the purpose of developing the leadership capabilities of the Executive Boards.

She has also been invited by the BBC as spokesperson in debates on coaching, is widely published in academic and non-academic literature and is the author of a number of books. Angélique has also been a member of both the Executive as well as the Advisory Boards of the European and Mentoring Coaching Council (EMCC) for five years. She was also the Editor for the *International Journal of Mentoring and Coaching* published by the EMCC for three years and is on the Editorial Board of a number of international journals. Her various roles have given her the opportunity to play a significant part in the emerging profession by influencing the setting of standards of coaching internationally.

ACKNOWLEDGEMENTS

The journey to complete this book faced a number of delays due to unforeseen obstacles and personal challenges. I am very grateful to Sage and my Editors, Nina Smith and Kirsty Smy, for their support during the process of getting this book to print. I doubt if I would have stayed the pace without their encouragement. I also want to thank the coaches and coachees who participated in the research that led to the writing of this book. Above all I want to thank my husband, Laurence Davies, for his unfailing encouragement and inspiration in my endeavours.

INTRODUCTION

1

CHAPTER OBJECTIVES

- Set the scene
- The Coaching Cycle model
- Introducing the underlying ontology and epistemology of the text
- Outlining the structure of the text

SETTING THE SCENE

I invite you, the reader, to enter into a dialogue with me for the purpose of making sense of coaching. You may share some of the ideas I put forward and you will no doubt also hold views that differ from mine. In the pages to follow I hope I will be able to contribute to your understanding of coaching and challenge some of the assumptions you may currently hold as to the nature of coaching. Coaching as a developing field remains in its infancy, both in terms of research as well as its practice. The diversity of techniques and intellectual traditions that underpin its disparate practices reflects the eclectic views on what constitutes coaching. It is for this reason that coaching is perceived as having a long way to go in establishing itself as a profession (Brockbank and McGill, 2006; Cox et al., 2010). This can be perceived as both a strength and a weakness. The weakness is reflected in the questions raised from different quarters as to the credibility of the emerging profession. The strength is the immense flexibility of coaching, with its array of creative intervention strategies to meet the individual needs of the coachee. I will explore the tension between these two positions, namely the desire for proper professional status complete with agreed standards and the appeal offered by the freedom of manoeuvre, supported by a critical approach as put forward by postmodernism.

Coaching has its roots buried in education, psychology, therapy, counselling, sports coaching and organizational development, all contributing to the eclectic nature of coaching. The extant literature of coaching would suggest that it has developed along two parallel paths. One path favours the models- and techniques-based approach, with its assumptions based on the behaviourist tradition. This perspective is particularly evident in executive and management coaching, which is dominated by a need to achieve goals and objectives and bring about visible changes in behaviours (du Toit, 2010). However, this approach ignores the unconscious and cognitive elements that shape the behaviours and performance of individuals. The second path, according to Stober (2006), has its philosophical foundation based in a humanistic psychology with human growth and change at its core. Stober (2006) also suggests that many of the approaches to coaching, such as the person-centred approach, therapies that include practices such as Gestalt, existentialism and psychotherapy, all have their roots in the humanistic perspective. However, this perspective is embedded in a therapeutic environment that deals with varying levels of dysfunction and pathology whereas coaching endeavours to work with functional individuals with an emphasis on the future.

Irrespective of the approach to coaching, it requires deep reflection by both the coach and coachee and the necessity to explore the values and beliefs that drive the individual while at the same time having a consideration of the wider system in which the coachee operates. In the chapters to follow I put forward the argument that the transformational power of coaching needs to be much more informed by a critical perspective than has been the case hitherto. Within the coaching space the role of the coach is both to support and challenge the individual to engage in a process of retrospective sensemaking. It is often in the space of silence created by coaching that the individual is able to become aware of the very essence of who they are, the values and beliefs which drive their behaviours and the contribution they have made to the particular set of circumstances they find themselves in. I argue that coaching at the highest level challenges the participants to take responsibility and ownership for their role in any situation or experience they encounter. The coaching space therefore has the ability to challenge the rhetoric that has informed the reality the coachee is experiencing at a given time.

The audience for this book is first and foremost aimed at the systemic eclectic end of the mature or maturing coach as identified by Clutterbuck and Megginson (2011), who offer four stages of development for the aspiring coach to journey through. These are as follows:

1. Models-based coaches. This identifies the aspiring coach who sets off on their development journey and who seeks the comfort and security of tried and tested models. Their approach is mechanistic as the model drives the intervention and conversations with the client.
2. Process-based approach. There is more flexibility in the coach's approach and they draw on a number of different tools and techniques, although their repertoire remains limited. The approach continues to be wedded to a solutions focus.
3. Philosophy or discipline-based mindset. The coach begins to apply a much wider portfolio of responses to the needs of the client and their approach is identified by the ability to reflect on their practice.
4. The systemic eclectic. This is the most liberated approach and the coach has a wide-ranging portfolio that includes knowledge and expertise from different disciplines. Their approach is non-mechanistic and they have internalized the array of tools and techniques which enables them to identify the most appropriate approach to meet the needs of the client.

However, for those of you embarking on the coaching journey and currently at the beginning of exploring what coaching might mean to you, the debates I put forward in this text will give you an alternative view of coaching and one mainly based on an underlying philosophy of coaching. This book therefore does not offer any new tools or techniques, nor does it favour any one in particular. It does, however, endeavour to explain what transpires within the coaching space, irrespective of the technique or approach employed by the coach. It aims to transcend the mechanistic input of coaching and instead addresses the black box of coaching; the conversion of the intervention strategy which leads to the output. The assertions are supported by vignettes offered by individuals and their particular experiences of coaching, whether as a coach or coachee.

There has been an explosion of the coaching literature in recent years. Whatever the desired outcome there are a vast array of existing and growing models and techniques put forward with which to achieve these outcomes. This text will focus on the theories and concepts not hitherto associated with coaching, but which helps to explain the process between the inputs and the outputs. This text therefore transcends the need to engage in what Clutterbuck and Megginson (2011) define as the motivations of different schools of thought who seek to marginalize the views of alternative approaches, which in my view is counter-productive and serves no purpose other than to discredit the profession. I believe that any of the models and techniques thus far promoted in the literature all have a place in the toolbox of the coach. The challenge arises when any of these is hailed as the holy grail of coaching. As Clutterbuck and Megginson (2011) point out, the truly mature coach is able to elegantly and seamlessly select the right tool or technique for the specific situation presented by the coachee or, in certain circumstances, no tool at all. The structure of the book is guided by the model described below which reflects the key stages of coaching as I perceive it.

COACHING AND MENTORING

Some readers will no doubt come to the subject of coaching with the unanswered question as to the differences and similarities between coaching and mentoring and I suggest it would be of value to attend to this question at the outset. Two of the key authoritative figures on coaching and mentoring, Clutterbuck and Megginson (2005: 14), suggest that any attempts at polarizing coaching and mentoring is, in their terms, 'futile, and undermines the credibility of both coaching and mentoring'. Furthermore, the subject of coaching is dynamic and constantly in the process of changing and evolving, and I share the view of the authors that any attempt at categorizing coaching and mentoring is unhelpful. As Garvey et al. (2009) identify, there are distinct schools of thought in both camps and some of these vigorously protect their respective territories.

The reference, both directly and indirectly, to mentoring can be traced back thousands of years, beginning with Plato and Aristotle with some tentative links to classical times associated with coaching, namely that of Socrates and the Socratic dialogue in particular. I conclude the brief foray into the debate of the distinction between coaching and mentoring by suggesting that there is probably more that unites rather than separates the two practices. Any attempt at providing a definitive position on the differences or similarities between coaching and mentoring is beyond the scope or purpose of this book. The discussions and debates that follow are therefore levelled at the practice of coaching, some of which will no doubt apply to mentoring as well.

THE COACHING CYCLE

The following model, which I suggest goes some way to define the coaching process, acts as a map by which the book is structured. The first stage of the coaching journey is defined by identifying the client or clients and establishing a contract for the duration of the coaching relationship. The contract should include the agreed outcomes and should determine specific and clear boundaries as to the type of coaching, how a successful outcome will be achieved, identify the expectations of different stakeholders, etc. This stage should also reflect the particular approach and underlying philosophy of the coach. As will be discussed in subsequent chapters, there are many routes into the provision of the coaching intervention and it is important for both the coach and coachee that there is clarity about the particular approach and the tools and techniques that might be employed.

Stage two of the coaching journey is what I define as the 'black box' of coaching. The focus of the existing literature seems to be on either the inputs, namely the models and techniques with the GROW model as probably the most well known, or the outputs, i.e. performance and achievement of goals. There appears to be little by way of addressing the stage in between and its contribution to what would be identified as coaching. As there is an absence in the literature on making this stage explicit, it remains an enigma – a black box that is complex and difficult to define. It is for this reason that this book deliberately excludes the positioning of different models or techniques. There are other texts that specifically provide a description of the various approaches available to the coach and the endless models and techniques associated with various traditions. Instead, the purpose is to focus on the actual process of coaching in an attempt to make the black box more transparent.

As one coachee mentioned to me, it is a 'sacred space or bubble', which is not necessarily defined by a physical place but rather refers to a psychological space that can equally be established within a busy public place or a quiet environment dedicated to coaching. It is also seen as a place the coachee can return to in their mind during the periods between the actual coaching sessions. Irrespective of the approach or techniques employed by the coach, I will suggest that certain key practices are associated with this stage of the coaching process and these will be discussed at length throughout the book. The final stage is identified as the outputs of the coaching intervention, which will, of course, be different for different individuals although there appears to be some common benefits identified by coachees. Irrespective of the individual benefits, one such common theme is that of personal development and change.

PHILOSOPHY OF THE COACH

I will argue throughout the book that it is necessary for coaching to be supported by an overall philosophy on behalf of the coach. As I perceive it as the underpinning of the coaching practice, irrespective of the models or techniques an individual coach employs, I will begin my discussions with exploring how philosophy can inform the practice drawing on some examples for discussion. Having an overarching philosophy to one's practice of coaching allows for congruence in how the coach engages in their practice and it enables the coach to navigate through the sometimes challenging and turbulent waters encountered during the coaching intervention. One such philosophy, which I argue is well suited to the practice of coaching, is that of scepticism, which has its roots in critical theory and which I discuss in depth in Chapter 3.

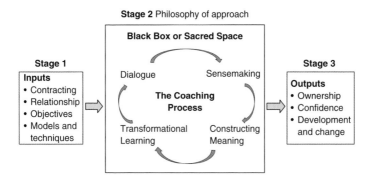

FIGURE 1.1   The Coaching Cycle, adapted from du Toit (2010)

Unlike many other discourses, which allow the researcher, author and reader to indulge in the joy of pure intellectual debate and pontification, coaching is the application of the many theories and concepts that have all played a role in shaping what we have come to understand as coaching. Unlike the student of many other subjects, learners on various coaching programmes are engaged in the learning journey for the express purpose of becoming a better and more developed coach. The applied application of theory has been a passion of mine and has underpinned the long journey of learning I embarked on many years ago and which supports all my activities, whether it is coaching, research, writing, designing of programmes or engaging in debates at conferences. I have therefore endeavoured to address the needs of both the academic community, drawing on relevant theories and concepts supported by the appropriate references. At the same time

I have also endeavoured to demonstrate how these ideas could inform the practice of coaching and to provide a map to the potential coachee who wants to better understand what coaching may or may not offer them.

ORGANIZATION OF THE BOOK

The book is organized in the following chapters.

Chapter 2 provides a critical overview of the current coaching literature for the purpose of positioning the ideas that follow within current thinking and practices of coaching. It is true to say that coaching has been greatly influenced by psychology, but it remains without wider philosophical principles to underpin its practice. The practice of coaching that has received most attention and focus has been executive and business coaching with the explicit goal of seeking to improve the performance of the individual and the organization. Coaching has yet to address wider social debates, challenging the fundamental and corresponding social beliefs that underpin and condone organizational practices. Instead, it has historically reflected the organizational obsession with performance and goals or on the opposite end of the continuum, life coaching, which in its extreme is devoid of challenge and realism.

To lend credibility and substance to coaching, many of the models and concepts have been borrowed and adopted from psychology. Psychology has traditionally focused on the disease within individuals and groups, seeking ways of 'fixing' what is perceived to be wrong with the individual. There is a lack of reference to a wider philosophical underpinning to truth and reality in both the literature as well as the practice of coaching, which I endeavour to address in this text.

Chapter 3 introduces the role of philosophy in coaching and that of critical theory in particular, which promotes the virtues of scepticism. As I perceive the support of a coaching philosophy to be fundamental to the personal approach of the coach, I begin the journey of exploration of what coaching is with a debate and discussion as to the contribution of philosophy to the practice of coaching. The sceptical bias of recent critical theories, namely that of poststructuralism and postmodernism, is introduced and its implications for coaching are emphasized. Scepticism particularly encourages radical and ongoing assessment of belief systems and their received wisdom; the dominant ideology. Of significance to coaching is the emphasis of difference in poststructuralist thought. Poststructuralist thinkers challenge the perceived homogeneity subscribed to by those in power and instead argue that the world around us was characterized by difference. This is a point of view shared by postmodernism, which sets out to undermine the grand narratives of our culture. Jean-François Lyotard in particular encouraged the rejection of institutional authority, suggesting that it invariably includes the suppression of divergent viewpoints. Psychologically this may be challenging to an individual who prefers to stay loyal to the status quo due to the emotional energy that has been invested in particular institutions, such as an organization, over the years. Coaching supported by critical theory provides the mechanism by which such power structures can be challenged. Critical theory is rich in concepts enabling the user to construct new narratives thereby furthering the debate in a particular field.

As we argue in our book, a coaching practice more geared to scepticism would be a significant step towards challenging the fundamentalism that has created so many problems in the business world at the time of writing (du Toit and Sim, 2010). One of the key values of coaching is that it is powerful in assisting the individual to address both their own internal barriers as well as the collective barriers that exist in organizations. Coaching addresses the worldview of the individual and their place in that world. Coaching offers the mechanism through which to challenge the stories and narratives that come to dominate an organization and, by default, the behaviours of those within it. In order to develop a sceptical attitude the coach is able to draw on a rich tradition of thought in this area, including that of contemporary postmodernism which is committed to the scrutiny of authority, its assumptions and practices. Furthermore, the coachee is encouraged to examine their beliefs with a view to seeing what lies behind them and whether they are more than tradition or habit. Asking the awkward questions helps the coachee to foster an enquiring mind at all times.

Chapter 4 discusses the prerequisites that contribute to the power of coaching. Before we even embark on the coaching itself, we need to contract both with the coachee as well as any other stakeholders, such as the line manager, Human Resources and the organization itself. The contracting process will help the coach in dealing with the sometimes tricky question of who is the coachee. The success of any coaching intervention is dependent on the quality of the relationship between the coach and coachee and the dialogue they engage in within the coaching space. A further key aspect of a successful coaching relationship is the ability of the coach to develop a high level of trust with the coachee. As with many journeys, the coaching journey also takes the participants into the unknown, which may feel scary and at the same time messy. The trust the coach and coachee establish provides the comfort and support for the coachee to continue on this unknown journey of discovery. The trust is also important as it legitimizes the time, space and commitment of the coachee to the process and it also offers their support in entering the unknown. The trust experienced by the coachee goes beyond the contractual relationship between the coach and coachee, and reflects more of a psychological contract. Although it is relatively absent from the coaching literature, Rogers (1967, 1980) has written extensively on the value of the relationship, as outlined in his person-centred approach in counselling and learning. This chapter will identify the value and importance of creating the relationship between the coach and coachee and the setting up of the space for reflection necessary for the benefits of coaching to be realized. A key component not often discussed in the literature is the readiness of the coachee to be coached. Identifying the willingness to engage with the process will be part of the contracting as well as establishing the psychological contract.

The coaching space is the container within which the coaching takes place. It needs to be consciously created by the coach, and one way to achieve this, as I will argue, is the presence of the coach. Coaching legitimizes the space to think, which is perceived as one of the most important benefits of coaching. Coaching provides both a mental as well as a psychological space in which people can explore what is important to them. It is not necessarily a physical space, but a 'sacred space' that facilitates deep thinking and reflection. The emphasis is on inner learning where constructs about self and others are questioned, often resulting in inner struggles. The process involves values, feelings, ideals and often moral decision-making and the exploring of self-concepts. It is argued that this process addresses the subjective world of the coachee, challenging their taken-for-granted assumptions about themselves and their world. There are a number of pre-requisites to ensure the quality and depth of such thinking which is explored in this chapter.

Chapter 5 introduces the key principles of sensemaking, which is depicted as the process through which people reduce the complexity of their environment to a level from which they can make sense. The chapter will discuss the ideas of sensemaking as a meaning-creating activity put forward by Weick (1979, 1995). It is the process through which various kinds of information, insights and ideas coalesce into something useful and come together in a meaningful way. A fundamental assumption of sensemaking is that of a process involving the social construction of reality. Retrospection is also an intimate part of the process of sensemaking and reflects how the coach supports the coachee to make sense of their issues and context retrospectively. Sensemaking suggests that people learn about who they are by projecting themselves into their environment and gaining insight from the feedback this generates. People therefore both react to and are shaped by their environment whilst influencing and contributing to the surroundings they experience. The reflective space provided by coaching facilitates the sensemaking process as described.

It is suggested that sensemaking is an ongoing, retrospective activity a person engages in collectively within their relationships or communities of practice. The sense they make of a particular event or situation will in turn influence future sensemaking activities. It is through stories that the individual shares the sense made, thereby creating a collective and shared understanding of reality as perceived at a particular time. As soon as a person becomes aware of an experience it is already in the past; it is the retrospective action of capturing a moment in the continuous flow of the present. Sensemaking is also reliant on dealing with equivocality rather than certainty. The ability to make sense of new situations may very well require the sense-maker to disrupt beliefs based on previous sensemaking, which is an assumed outcome of the coaching process. Sensemaking is also described as a process without beginning or end; it is a continuous flow of meaning creation. The person is constantly revising and building provisional assumptions. Sensemaking as an ongoing activity enacted through conversation, storytelling, narration, linguistic abilities, suggests that they all play a part in the process of making sense of the complexity and ambiguity the coachee operates in.

Chapter 6 draws on the theories of narrative and storytelling, which have received much attention from organizational scholars in recent years. This chapter will build on the previous chapter on sensemaking, which suggests that it is through stories that we make sense of our environment and experiences. Some of the main proponents of storytelling who inform this chapter are Boje (1995, 2008; Boje et al., 1999) and Gabriel (2004). The narrative approach draws on a history through which philosophers and scientists endeavour to understand the ways we come to know what we know. Narrative and storytelling are underpinned by a key assumption that reality is constructed as a story and which social actors are constantly rewriting through a collective process. Furthermore, the narrative paradigm advocates that people come to know what they know by telling stories of personal experiences in different settings, such as the setting provided by the coaching space. It is through the rewriting of their stories and the redefinition of their experiences and supported by the transformational process of coaching, that frames of references are adapted.

Storytelling is a complex process as there are multiple interacting stories unfolding simultaneously. Individuals are participating in their own life story, the story of their organizations, communities and families concurrently, with each story influencing the other. The history of storytelling is as rich and varied as the history of mankind and perceived as the most widely used means of communication. Storytelling combines perceived facts with emotions, ideas, values and norms. Through the telling of our stories are we able to organize events, thereby establishing coherence. It makes the communication of abstract ideas and behaviours possible, creating shared expectations and interpretation. Storytelling has a relatively long history in its contribution to learning and meaning construction. Through the use of stories, the coachee is also able to make sense of and experiment with an alternative past, present and future. Storytelling also allows the coachee to understand how their story is influenced by the many stories of others they are interconnected with.

Chapter 7 introduces a constructionist perspective, which suggests that we are the authors of our own stories. The objective of the book is to move away from a performance-led, psychology-biased approach to coaching to one based on critical principles drawing on theories of constructionism as outlined by Gergen (1999, 2001; Gergen and Gergen, 2008), Bruner (1986, 1990, 1991) and Burr (1995). A constructionist perspective challenges people to be ever-vigilant and critical of their assumptions and assumed truths about the world. A constructionist perspective argues that knowledge is not discovered, but rather constructed within a relational environment of shared experiences and understandings. A social constructionist philosophy encourages the individual or group to be open to possibilities and to reconstruct reality through a process of continuous reflection. It also carries with it the burden of responsibility for the reality created, which must constantly be subjected to sceptical scrutiny. Without scrutiny individuals are constrained into maintaining the status quo.

According to constructionism, reality does not exist independently of the individual. An appreciation of the world is seen as being dependent from an understanding of how an individual shapes the world internally. The social world is therefore perceived as the product of social construction by the individuals within society, a process that is of an ongoing nature. Furthermore, adherents to this paradigm do not believe social reality to have an independent existence outside the consciousness of individuals and perceives the ontological status of the social world as being questionable. Every human situation is considered novel and emergent and filled with multiple, and often-times conflicting, meanings and interpretations. An overriding purpose of coaching is, as will be argued in previous chapters, to support the coachee in making sense of such ambiguity.

As the lived world is continuously changing, meaning can only be achieved through participation in the world. The participative nature of the constructionist paradigm is contrary to the positivistic paradigm which considers the observer to be detached from the world. Instead, constructionism endeavours to understand the world of interactive relationships that connect individuals into webs of meaningful experience. The acceptance of a multiplicity of reality is encompassed within this paradigm. The primary interest of approaching coaching from this paradigm is the quest to understand the subjective experience of the coachee and is supportive of the theoretical assumptions of the other proposed chapters.

Chapter 8 introduces the assumption of this book that coaching is also a journey of discovery and learning. There is much diversity amongst researchers as to what constitutes learning. It is suggested that learning can be understood as a change in the behaviour of the learner as learning facilitates a modification or addition to existing behaviours. Adult learning is seen as complex and multidimensional, involving an understanding of meaning and self-knowledge gained through critical reflection. Transformative learning promotes a learning environment in which the learner plays an active role in their own learning. The result is that teacher and learner collaborate in the process of constructing meaning. Learning therefore becomes a reciprocal experience for the learner and teacher. This equally reflects the practice and experiences of the coaching process. Some of the proponents informing this chapter are Knowles (1980), Cranton (1996), Dirkx (2001), Mezirow (1990, 1991, 1994, 1996, 1997), Brockbank and McGill (2006).

The traditional approach to learning defines it as a process whereby the individual gained knowledge and skills and possibly also attitudes and opinions. However, in recent years learning has increasingly been seen as a social process that takes place in the interaction between people, resulting in the constructionist view of learning. Transformational learning is defined as inner learning where constructs about self and others are questioned, often resulting in inner struggles. Furthermore, adult learning involves values, feelings, ideals and often moral decision-making and the exploring of self-concepts. It is argued that such learning addresses the subjective world of the learner, challenging their taken-for-granted assumptions about the world – which is an expected outcome of the coaching intervention. The theories of transformational, adult learning reflect the discussions of constructionism, sensemaking and storytelling introduced in previous chapters.

Chapter 9 draws together the various theoretical concepts introduced, which would ultimately lead to the outputs of coaching – the final stage of my proposed model of coaching. There is a sense that the coach does not offer solutions, but instead emphasizes the need for the individual to take ownership for their own development and any changes they may want to bring about in their circumstances. The notion of ownership is also a major theme of transformative learning as we will have seen in the previous chapter. Other than the gift of ownership, coaching also results in empowerment and the confidence of the coachee to make any change to their situation or circumstances, if they so choose.

The chapters described above are interactive and a coachee may journey through them a number of times throughout the coaching experience. The chapters refer to the experience of coaching identified in the 'black box' referred to in the introductory chapter. The coaching process as addressed throughout therefore puts forward a new heuristic of coaching as a process of sensemaking constructed between the coach and coachee and which is achieved through dialogue resulting in transformational learning.

And now, let us begin the exploration of the black box of coaching ...

AN OVERVIEW OF THE COACHING LITERATURE

2

CHAPTER OBJECTIVES

- Explore the current literature on coaching
- Identify the different schools of coaching
- Offer a critical view of the strengths and weaknesses
- Establish the gaps in the literature

INTRODUCTION

As supported by Downey (2003), a review of the literature reveals that coaching means different things to different people. Furthermore, each coach will approach coaching from a position that would reflect their own preference for a particular style which will be dependent on their personal experience, education and biases. This is reinforced by Whybrow (2008), who asserts that there is no standardized approach to coaching. Ideally, the coach has to adapt their style according to the needs and circumstances of the coachee, which is not always evident, as I discuss later. The lack of evidence-based research of coaching and the absence of an overall code of practice leads to criticisms such as those posed by Grant (2007), which go on to question whether coaching is not merely a more socially acceptable form of therapy. Price (2009) points out that the lack of clarity as to what constitutes coaching may also lead to a difficulty in identifying the boundaries between coaching and other interventions such as counselling or therapy. The result is that coaches might inadvertently stray into areas and situations they are not equipped to deal with (Nelson and Hogan, 2009). Such a scenario may pose an ethical dilemma for the coach, which is one example of the need for establishing a clear contract with the client from the outset. The contract should clearly specify the expectations of the relationship, the approach to be used and the expected outcomes.

As a new and unregulated profession, an ethical framework is patchy, and unless the coach is a member of one of the coaching associations, it is likely that they would be unaware of any ethical guidelines. Coaches themselves find it difficult to articulate clearly and specifically the properties of coaching and how these are reflected in their practice. Instead, Askeland (2009) proposes that coaches often turn to the mystical, arguing that it cannot be explained, but instead has to be experienced. Chapman et al. (2003) go so far as to suggest that coaching is both a science and an art. Grant (2007) is not perturbed by the diversity that marks coaching and perceives it to be a strength and not a liability. One of the benefits is the flexibility and creativity it affords the coach, allowing them to draw on the tools and techniques best suited to the specific situation and client need. Bachkirova (2007) raises a valid concern in the absence of a clear definition of coaching, namely that it makes it difficult in identifying the criteria by which a reputable coach may be judged. The route to coaching is therefore varied and diverse. Some coaches have a background in psychology or therapy whereas others were business consultants, managers or human resource practitioners in a previous career. Some might even be retired directors who, due to their knowledge of business, see it is an opportunity to make their experience available to others; and so the list goes on.

Irrespective of the differences in the coaching approach, the common theme is that coaching is a didactic relationship entered into by the coach and coachee for the purpose of developing the personal performance of the client (Stober, 2008; Witherspoon and White, 1996). Brockbank and McGill (2006: 9) clearly state that, 'coaching has one clear purpose, the learning and development of an individual, a process that involves change'. (The theme of coaching and learning will be explored at length in Chapter 8.) The preferred discourse influencing the practice of the coach, such as leadership development, learning or psychology, will determine the models and the techniques the coach will select in their practice of coaching. John Whitmore suggests during an interview with Kauffman (2008) that coaching as an industry is better placed than any other to support individuals in working towards taking more responsibility for their lives. This view is supported by Stober (2006), who argues that the humanistic influence on coaching encourages coaches to hold their clients accountable for the choices they make and the responsibility associated with those choices. Wilson (2007) is of the same opinion and perceives the agenda of the intervention to be driven by the coachee, who therefore has the ultimate say in the outcome of the process.

It is, however, an accountability that is without blame and judgement. Instead, it supports the coachee in identifying different choices in different circumstances and what they may want to change or do differently in particular areas of their lives. A person-centred perspective suggests that for an individual to achieve self-actualization they need the right environment, which requires an acceptance of the coachee as they are, without judgement. Instead, the coach is there to listen and challenge without a personal agenda. This is one of the key tenets of a humanistic approach (Stober, 2006). The relationship is therefore rather unique. I suggest that many relationships come with an agenda; even in the most loving and caring of relationships there is an agenda as the best is sought for the other person. Although a friend may very well act as a sounding board, having someone listen to you without seeking personal gain or without a personal agenda, is much more liberating. A friend may very well collude with the person and tell them what they want to hear without challenging their assumptions and points of view. The fine balance between support and challenge is possibly what leads to the view of coaching being both a science and an art. In the following section I identify some of the key themes of coaching, which are either extensively pursued, hinted at or ignored within the literature.

MODELS AND TECHNIQUES

There is a plethora of models and techniques at the disposal of the coach, and as Kemp (2008) points out, the GROW model attributed to John Whitmore (Whitmore, 1996) is probably the most widely recognized and adopted model within the coaching community. It is increasingly only one of a growing collection of coaching models. There is, however, a lack of empirical evidence to support the efficacy of the GROW model and some of the critique levied against it questions its simplicity and theoretical flaws and an absence of consistent and reproducible theory (Kemp, 2008). Continuing the challenge, Passmore (2007) suggests one of the reasons for its success is because it is supported by reward and punishment, which remains prevalent within organizations. I introduce the role of philosophy to coaching in the next chapter and, as we will see, a postmodernist perspective poses the challenge that favouring one model over others represents a belief in a metanarrative of coaching. What this means will become clear in the next chapter.

Simplistically put, Cope (2004) places many of the coaching models and techniques in one of two camps. On the one end of the continuum is an assumption that coaching is a process of transference of knowledge, meaning and understanding and therefore not coachee-led. (Transference in this instance does not refer to the psychological meaning of transference whereby one person unconsciously redirects feelings onto another individual.) On the other end of the continuum is the assumption that coaching is a process of discovery, helping the client to help themselves. Cope (2004) goes on to suggest that the coach does not impart any wisdom or knowledge. Instead their purpose is to bring out the best within the coachee. As introduced earlier, the purpose of coaching is to empower the coachee in a non-directive way. This is reflected in the view of De Haan and Burger (2005), who state that coaching provides the process which enables an individual to reflect on their own actions and thoughts for the purpose of identifying alternative ways of being and behaving.

Given the diversity of what constitutes coaching, is it any wonder that it is so difficult to measure the value and effectiveness of coaching with the multitude of models and techniques at the disposal of the coach? It also makes it nearly impossible to justify its use above that of other intervention practices such as facilitation or training. These issues make the drive for an overarching framework by which coaching is regulated an advantage. However, on the other hand there is a danger that coaches will focus on the framework and lose the creativity and flexibility to draw on the tools and techniques appropriate for a particular client with a particular need at a given time. In view of the significant consequences of regulation, I return to this debate in subsequent sections.

PERFORMANCE VS DEVELOPMENTAL COACHING

Brockbank and McGill (2006) went some way in devising a map with which to identify the different approaches to coaching, which supports the argument I put forward in this text, namely the value of a philosophy to provide a theoretical base to coaching. According to their map, a subjectivist view assumes that social realities like learning and development are fundamentally different from natural phenomena and can therefore not be captured by objective instruments, which on the other hand is the assumption of the objective dimension. Instead, the social world of the coachee is understood to be continuously constructed, reproduced and transformed through interaction with others. The personal and social world of the client is acknowledged as the basis of the developmental process. This particular style of coaching recognizes the socially constructed nature of reality.

It is a given within the business community in particular, that the purpose of coaching is to bring about changes in behaviours which will change and improve performance (Wilson, 2007). However, Silsbee (2008) challenges this assumption by arguing that performance coaching has its limitations. He goes on to suggest that it is often driven by organizational objectives, which may lead to tension between the objectives of the organization and that of the coachee. This poses one of the fundamental questions in coaching, namely who is the client? This is not always clear, which may present the coach with an ethical dilemma resulting from conflicting loyalties. The caring professions are clear on this point and perceive the needs and interests of the client to be the main priority. It is, however, more complex within an organizational setting where the needs of different stakeholders have to be considered, especially when the organization pays the bill. Continuing the challenge of performance coaching, Silsbee (2008) suggests that it can make learning more difficult as the implied standard of performance may create a tension in the perceived performance gap within the client. Instead, he argues that for new skills and competencies to be sustained, they need to be grounded in self-awareness and self-generation. Garvey (2011) supports this notion and argues that organizations are preoccupied with performance. He goes on to suggest that the focus on self-efficacy and learning will result in the enhancement of performance.

The inclusion of performance in organizational coaching can be traced to the influence of sports coaching, and many successful sporting people transfer the concepts of sporting performance into business and executive coaching. The reason for the lack of the desired performance improvement based on a goal or target approach is that at the heart of coaching is the assumption that it is for the purpose of developing the whole person as opposed to specific skills or competencies (Garvey, 2011). Furthermore, given the complexity of human nature, it is an erroneous view which suggests that human performance can be measured in such a simplistic and linear manner. The value of coaching is that it emphasizes learning versus performance and this proposal is discussed in greater detail in subsequent chapters.

In essence, Garvey et al. (2009) suggest that coaching is about change. This is supported by Peterson (2006), who argues that the purpose of coaching is to change behaviour. However, for change to be sustained the consensus amongst different proponents is that it is necessary for the coachee to learn how to coach themselves. The value of coaching therefore continues beyond that of the coaching relationship. Skiffington and Zeus (2003) suggest that coaching supports the way in which we interpret situations, which will in turn influence our behaviours in response to other situations. This reflects the sensemaking process put forward by Weick and discussed in depth in Chapter 4. This assumption is supported by Peltier (2009), who suggests that understanding the filters through which we interpret and judge events and situations will allow us to have deeper insight to our drivers, giving us more choice in our responses. If we are therefore able to change our cognitions we will also be able to bring about changes in our behaviours (Dobson and

Block, 1988; Dobson and Dozois, 2001). This leads to a discussion on the influence psychology has had in determining the models, processes and techniques applied within the coaching repertoire.

THE PSYCHOLOGY OF COACHING

The theme of psychology in coaching is a significant one and it is evident from the literature that humanistic psychology is the bedrock on which many coaching approaches are built. This statement is supported by Stober (2006), who suggests that humanistic psychology provides the foundation for many of the coaching models, especially in terms of the values and assumptions that underpin them. Whybrow (2008) puts forward the argument that psychology is deemed to be at the forefront in the development of coaching. This argument is supported by Linley and Harrington (2007), who purport that any of the numerous psychological practices is underpinned by a fundamental and deep-seated assumption of human nature. Bluckert (2005) goes further and argues that coaches need to possess a level of psychological skills and competencies to equip them in dealing effectively across the range of coaching scenarios they are likely to encounter. He adds that the term 'psychological-mindedness' has crept into the coaching literature and describes it as the top level competency for executive coaches in particular. It is defined as the ability to go beyond the obvious and to consider the causes and meanings of the behaviour, feelings and thoughts of the coachee. On the other hand, Garvey et al. (2009) point out that exposure to psychological training is not the only route to self-awareness and suggest that the various principles of adult-learning also result in a higher sense of self.

There is a counter-argument to the one that suggests coaches should not enter too far into the realms of psychology which suggests that, given the need for fast results and the achievement of outcomes, particularly within an organizational context, this makes it impractical. There are numerous theorists who support Hart et al. (2001) in their suggestion that there is considerable overlap between coaching, counselling and therapy. They go so far as to suggest that therapy shares similar theoretical constructs and practices as coaching. As suggested earlier, the common focus is based on a confidential, one-to-one or didactic relationship for the purpose of change. However, in therapy the focus of attention is often on interpersonal health and an identifiable issue such as depression which impacts on the ability of the individual to function. By contrast, as discussed above, the focus of the coach is on the untapped potential of the whole person, seeking to maximize their fulfilment in life and work. Whybrow (2008) contributes to the argument and suggests an additional added value offered by the psychology and therapy professions is an understanding of ethics and boundary management.

There is much evidence of a person-centred approach to psychology to be found in coaching. For example, it is based on an assumption that the coach is not the expert and that the purpose of coaching is to facilitate the self-determination of the coachee with the ultimate objective of optimal functioning. Joseph and Bryant-Jefferies (2007) go further and suggest that the starting point is irrelevant. However, the blurring of the boundaries between coaching and psychology may provide the coach with a challenge in maintaining the boundaries between psychology and coaching and, when engaged in coaching, not to intervene as a psychologist or therapist. De Haan and Burger (2005) are much more explicit in their assertion, which suggests that psychotherapy is influential in providing much of the roots that underpin coaching. This has led to what De Haan and Burger (2005: 52) identify as four distinct approaches to coaching. First is directive coaching, which focuses on improvement from the outside. Secondly is the person-centred approach, which attempts to shift the focus internally. The third approach is coaching from an analytical perspective, which is aimed at understanding from the inside. Finally, there is paradoxical coaching, which focuses on upsetting, surprising and manipulating from the outside.

Fundamentally, the influence of psychology on coaching is seen to enhance development in both the personal and professional life of the individual (Grant, 2007; Grant and Palmer, 2002). This is achieved through the application of well established psychological approaches of behavioural science. An example offered by de Vries et al. (2007) advocates that, as with psychology or therapy, coaching explores the blind spots and defensive routines of the coachee that may lead to distorted thinking. Whybrow (2008) contends that coaching psychology is based on the assertion that the individual is autonomous and capable of learning and reflective practice. The argument for a psychology of coaching is that much within the contemporary models of coaching originates from the humanistic movement of the 1960s, and is therefore seen as inherently being person-centred (Kauffman, 2008; Linley and Harrington, 2007; Whybrow, 2008).

Behaviourism has had its own influence on coaching and also draws on humanistic aspects, focusing on the building of rapport, creating empathy with the coachee and taking a non-judgemental stance towards the coachee. Coaching psychology also equips the coach to support the coachee to reflect on past experiences, bringing these to conscious awareness (Passmore, 2007). Palmer and Szymanska (2007) introduce a cognitive behavioural approach, which suggests that it enables the coachee to achieve realistic goals as well as improve performance. A cognitive approach is also perceived to develop psychological resilience, prevents stress and supports the coachee to overcome barriers to change. Furthermore, it also encourages the individual to reflect on beliefs that may lead to actions and behaviours that the coachee persists in pursuing despite a negative outcome. In turn it supports a coachee to develop a more balanced perspective to their strengths and weaknesses. The long history of well-established theories and practices which underpins psychology has been for the express purpose of understanding human development and behaviour. Supporting the argument for psychology to take the lead in establishing a meta-model of coaching is the fact that it is underscored by statistics and evidence-based research. However, such research practices have not yet reached the scrutiny of the coaching profession (Palmer and Whybrow, 2007). Furthermore, I concur with the challenges put forward by Garvey (2011: 87) that psychology has based its foundations of research on a positivistic, cause-and-effect philosophy. He identifies three major problems with this model of research, namely:

1. The researcher is neutral and objective.
2. It is important to isolate variables in order to know what you are testing.

3. Coaching, mentoring and psychotherapy are not static, they are dynamic processes and change occurs all the time.

As Garvey (2011) purports, neutrality and objectivity in human nature is a mirage. It is also virtually impossible to isolate variables in human activity. Furthermore, positivism perceives human relationships as static and does not take into account the dynamic and changing nature of relationships. I will in a later chapter discuss further the notion of humans as social beings whose identities, values, beliefs, feelings and behaviours are influenced by their social environment. The way to understand the human condition is therefore through the inclusion of an understanding of the context in which people find themselves and not through an attempt at controlling the human dynamic variable.

COACHING AND ORGANIZATIONS

Supporters of organizational coaching strongly argue that a competence in psychological methods is not enough within organizational coaching. Instead, Kampa-Kokesch and Anderson (2001) argue that a knowledge and awareness of business, business issues and leadership is necessary. This is supported by Spinelli (2008), who adds that an understanding of organizational and cultural discourses are equally important, which is also reinforced by Clutterbuck and Lane (2004) in relation to situational mentoring. One could argue that as organizations are focused on measurable outcomes that coaching within organizations would be driven by a need for solutions. As suggested earlier, there are those who question the goal-centric view of coaching, Kemp (2008) being among them.

Irrespective of the multiplicity of approaches, Brunning (2006) suggests that coaching has become the approach of choice in management and leadership development. As Gibb (2008) proposes, coaching allows the manager to explore, discover and clarify different ways of leading and developing. One of the reasons for the success of coaching within organizations is that it addresses deeply held beliefs and behaviours that inhibit the performance of the manager. Gibb (2008: 173) points out that, 'There is much in effective executive coaching that is about addressing core beliefs about self and abilities, and experimenting with new ways of being.' This is supported by Ducharme (2004), who proposes that the coachee will often seek help within a coaching environment to bring about changes in behaviours that are interfering with performance, such as changes in leadership styles. Unlike the therapeutic or counselling relationship, the coaching relationship is fairly short-term and arguably delivers high standards and goals. Furthermore, access to impartial support is not often available within organizations. Managers do not always have access to open and honest feedback from peers and others as to how their actions and behaviours are perceived externally. The coach is in the unique position of being able to ask the questions no one else in the organization would necessarily have the courage to ask.

In fact, Stober (2008) suggests that much of organizational coaching in recent years has been focused on leadership development. Downey (2003) perceives that coaching has an important contribution to make within organizations by reinstating humanity within the workplace. He goes on to suggest that this is achieved when the whole person is given the freedom to express themselves: their creativity, imagination, intelligence and pragmatism. Coaching also has the ability to support leaders in growing their emotional and relational capacity (Fillery-Travis and Lane, 2007; Kauffman, 2008). The expectation of emotional competence is increasingly being rated as the most important competency to develop en route to senior management positions (Wasylyshyn, 2003). De Vries et al. (2007) support the argument that emotions contribute to both our identities and behaviours and asserts that it is a combination of cognition and emotions which determines what we select to focus on or ignore. Wasylyshyn (2003) adds to the debate and posits that self-management allows the individual to control and manage disruptive emotions, adaptability, accountability and the recognition of when to act. According to de Vries et al. (2007) this self-awareness provides the individual with the tools to manage relationships and situations more effectively. Senior managers tend to be much more outwardly focused, certainly action-oriented and often motivated by power. Introspection does not always feature highly on their list of priorities. de Vries (1989) goes on to suggest that it is also a given that operating at the senior level of an organization can be lonely, with few people the senior executive can confide in or even share weaknesses and fears with. The coaching relationship provides them with the opportunity to do so safely and in confidence. Coaching focuses on communication at the inner tier which involves a much more personal and intimate level of communication. It is at this level that the manager is both challenged and given permission to deal with personal complexities, drivers and values which influence their ability to effectively communicate externally.

Increasingly organizations are seeking to create a coaching culture within their organizations and to establish the coaching capacity through the development of internal coaches. Such an endeavour not only offers advantages, but also poses challenges to the organization. Wilson (2007) points out some of the obvious ones, such as the reservations individuals would have about being coached by someone else in the organization due to seniority, confidentiality and reporting structures. The authors with the authority on creating a coaching culture, Clutterbuck and Megginson (2005), suggest that coaching has the potential of setting the tone of how relationships are managed throughout an organization. However, they go on to suggest that the case for creating a coaching culture is not going to be the same for every organization. Organizations that find themselves in the position of having to face continuous and oftentimes disruptive change will probably gain the most from establishing a coaching culture. Clutterbuck and Megginson (2005) add a further warning and suggest that not only does it require investment on the part of the organization, but commitment from the leadership is essential. In essence, 'a coaching culture demands a morally rigorous and humanistic approach to work and relationship' (Clutterbuck and Megginson, 2005: 19).

THE LIMITATIONS OF COACHING

A perceived weakness not of coaching, but of the recipients of coaching such as leaders and organizations, is their possible unwillingness to engage in a critical analysis of values, group norms, ideologies and associated behaviour. Such unwillingness is also evident in the selection of coaches. Coaches are not always selected for their ability to challenge the individual or organization, but possibly because they are perceived as being able to reinforce existing norms and practices. de Vries et al. (2007) suggest that clients may make a choice based on what they believe to be rational criteria, whereas in fact they may be influenced by the unconscious desire to find a coach who will not take them too far out of their 'comfort zone'. As discussed, much of organizational coaching is driven by a need for measurable goals and objectives which is challenged by numerous writers of coaching. Clutterbuck and Megginson (2011) point out that this may result in the coach manipulating the relationship in favour of their own agenda. For example, focusing on specific goals in the early stages of the coaching relationship may merely serve as a crutch for the coach rather than serve the needs of the coachee.

Earlier on I challenged the fact that many of the approaches to coaching, supported by the literature, are driven by an apparent obsession with creating tools and techniques rather than on establishing an underlying philosophy with which to support the tools and techniques. Brockbank and McGill (2006: 9) concur with the challenge that there is an apparent lack of a supporting philosophy underpinning the practice of many coaches and suggest that: 'Because the philosophy that underlies any approach will impact on its outcome, we recommend that practitioners take time to examine their philosophy, however embedded it might be, and make this known to prospective clients.' Instead, coaches are influenced by the current models deemed to be in fashion and which promise the solutions to all the issues brought to the coaching relationship by the coachee. Clutterbuck and Megginson (2011) are of the same mind and add that one of the dangers in a single model approach to coaching is that the coach may miss important clues revealed by the coachee, which would provide insight to their circumstances and context. There may also be the temptation on the part of the coach to manipulate the agenda to support their particular model or preferred approach.

Kemp (2008) offers his own criticisms of the claims associated with many of the coaching models. He suggests that despite the popularity of some of these models, many make erroneous claims of validity – claims supported by tenuous evidence that remains unfounded. Instead, Kemp (2008) argues that the purpose of these claims is to help coaches in differentiating themselves in an increasingly crowded marketplace. Garvey et al. (2009) concur and point out that the breadth and quality of available research in coaching remains fragmented and rudimentary. It is evident from the eclectic mix of books available on coaching that there is a plethora of models and techniques available to the coach. On the other hand, the absence of an overall framework with which to define coaching means it has not yet been possible to successfully and consistently measure the value and effectiveness of coaching. Measurement within organizations tends to favour quantitative data, yet the complexities of the coaching approach means that qualitative measures are possibly better suited in identifying the perceived value of coaching.

The person-centred view of coaching emphasizes the importance of approaching the coachee from a non-judgemental perspective for the purpose of encouraging self-determination and a motivation for them to achieve their optimal level of functioning (Joseph and Bryant-Jefferies, 2007). Such an approach raises interesting questions in relation to the willingness or effectiveness of the coach in being able to challenge behaviour that may have a detrimental effect on others as well as the wider system within which the individual operates. As suggested earlier, many of the models and techniques of coaching can be traced back to humanistic psychology. A possible blind spot of a humanistic philosophy might lead a coach to become too close to the coachee and their personal development needs, thereby colluding with the coachee and therefore failing to provide one of the key benefits of coaching, namely the ability to challenge and question their assumptions, values and behaviours. The benefit of critical thinking is therefore not only in providing rigour to the coaching practice, but also provides an added benefit to coaches. It challenges coaches to constantly question and reflect on their own practice and the assumptions that underpin it. In this way the coach will be able to provide the *tough love* associated with the value of the coaching intervention. The coaching relationship is not one of friendship as friends conspire with each other, reinforcing the worldview of the other without question for fear of upsetting the relationship. The non-judgemental support referred to in coaching does not mean the coach is blind to the weaknesses of the coachee. Instead it means the coach is there to inspire the coachee to develop a balanced self-awareness which includes both the coachee's strengths and weaknesses.

Continuing with the reservation of whether certain coaching approaches are equipped to challenge the values and beliefs of individuals and organizations, I turn to the increasing attempt by organizations to introduce a coaching culture. In support of my scepticism whether organizations are able to do so successfully, I turn to Clutterbuck and Megginson (2005: 2) who caution organizations attempting to establish a coaching culture, that '[a] coaching culture ... is an on-going commitment far more difficult to budget for. The financial cost is implicated by the need to change attitudes and practices that relate to just about every aspect of the business.' I voice concerns of an apparent lack of scepticism and suggest that the transformation of an individual or organization will only come about if existing views and the status quo are challenged. The reflective practice of coaching provides the coachee with the mechanism to question both their own prevailing paradigms as well as that of the organization within which they are embedded. I have significant reservations whether an internal coach, paid by the organization, will be in a position to do so effectively. In addition, the eclectic mix to coaching discussed above means that even within one organization there would possibly be numerous interpretations of coaching and therefore different coaching practices. One such example is the NHS, which has been committed to embedding coaching as a means of developing their staff. If the different Trusts approached coaching from their own particular brand and interpretation, there may very well be little consistency across the organization. The result would be confusion and a possible cynicism as to the value and need to promote coaching within the organization. On the other hand, as I argue in the next chapter, a metanarrative of coaching is also not necessarily the answer.

Established professions such as counselling and psychotherapy are regulated by a code of conduct, taking ethical issues into consideration. Coaching as a new and unregulated profession has yet to establish an ethical framework, which is patchy at best. The coach would have access to an ethical framework only if they were a member of one of the coaching associations. Furthermore, such ethical guidelines and frameworks are merely advisory and are not enforceable at present. The nature of coaching guarantees that at some stage during the practice of coaching, the coach will encounter a situation that will require the support and guidance of an ethical framework to resolve the issue. There are added complexities in relation to organizations and the provision of internal coaching. For example, the coach may become party to information that breaches organizational regulations and issues of loyalty may then arise.

A further question is how such information should be dealt with whilst at the same time protecting the contract of client confidentiality. How does the coach treat the information and knowledge they become party to within the confines of the coaching relationship? One route is for the coach to develop a philosophical framework that underpins their practice and approach to coaching. Another solution in overcoming some of the ethical dilemmas is by ongoing development of the coach through supervision. Research would suggest, however, that very few coaches engage in regular supervision sessions despite the obvious benefits. It would appear that there is an implicit assumption among newly qualified coaches that once they have completed their chosen programme of study, further development and supervision is no longer a priority. This is despite the fact that supervision would clearly provide the necessary support to any coach when dealing with the ethical complexities referred to above.

The supervision of the coach, whether a novice or a seasoned coach, is pivotal in the ongoing development of the professional coach, providing the coach with the support needed for raising their self-awareness as well as awareness of their practice. Supervision provides the coach with both professional development as well as opportunities for reflective learning. There are different ways the coach can obtain supervision, either on a one-to-one basis, in a group, or a combination of both. The advantage of peer supervision, which is facilitated by an experienced coach, allows participants to learn from each other and to explore different perspectives. Irrespective of the approach to supervision, it provides the vehicle through which the coach actively engages in the development of their practice and supports them in defining their particular brand of coaching. Unless an individual coach is part of an organization or a group of associates it can be lonely, and there will come a time in the career of any coach when they may be uncertain as to how effective they are being in meeting the needs of their clients. In order to benefit from the supervision, it is imperative that the coach engages in it regularly for the breadth and depth of their coaching practice and framework to be reviewed and developed.

Evidence of supervision practice provides assurance to the organization that any unethical or poor coaching is identified and improved upon. The supervisory approach scrutinizes the practice of the coach and identifies ways in which they can best meet the needs of their client and the organization. A coaching client is always part of a wider system and complexities that surround their various relationships and roles. The supervisor is a valuable and impartial support to the coach in identifying the dynamics and the influence on the client and how the client presents these during the coaching sessions. As mentioned earlier, the possibility of complex ethical issues arising is part of the milieu of coaching and the impartial perspective of the supervisor provides objective support in unravelling the complexity and sensitivity surrounding such situations. Supervision also provides the supportive space in which the coach can 'offload' their own issues with the same degree of non-judgemental acceptance afforded to the coachee. In order for the coach to compete successfully in an increasingly sophisticated and crowded market, supervision should not be seen as an optional extra but a competitive necessity.

TEAM COACHING

There has been a significant growth of team coaching in recent years. One could question whether the motivation is mainly financial as the cost would be considerably less than that of coaching the individuals in the team. One of the possible advantages of team coaching is that it may be well placed to address some of the relationship issues within a team. However, it is open for debate exactly what coaching is able to add over and above action learning or facilitation. There remain doubts as to whether team coaching actually exists or whether it is merely old wine in new bottles. Such scepticism is shared by Garvey et al. (2009), who question whether claims of developing a theory of team coaching have successfully been achieved, and whether it is capable of being distinguished from other approaches to group interventions.

The absence of critical reflection in the coaching community is shared by Askeland (2009), who delivers a sharp criticism when he suggests that the inability to put forward underlying theoretical assumptions makes it difficult to establish a credibility for coaching. Furthermore, the absence of critical reflection prevents the practice from measuring its successes as well as its limitations. One explanation might be that it is due to the fact that coaching has attracted professionals from a wide variety of disciplines as well as numerous sub-disciplines such as psychology, counselling and therapy, not to mention the various disciplines from business and management. On the one hand there are those who suggest that the absence of a common definition of coaching is damaging to the professionalism of coaching. On the other hand there are others who insist that coaching should not be judged on a common definition, but suggest instead that it is the outcome of the intervention that is important.

The overlap between the different disciplines that have contributed to coaching processes makes the regulation and consistency of a coaching approach problematic, despite calls for the need of regulation. In his latest book, Peltier (2009) succinctly summarizes these questions by saying: 'What is real? What is bogus? What is coaching and what is psychotherapy? Where does psychology fit into the coaching practice? Who should coach? And how?' Answers to these questions remain elusive. In the next chapter I outline why I propose that the emerging profession would benefit from the scepticism of critical thinking put forward by thinkers such as Jean-François Lyotard. A critical approach would provide the structure with which to debate the consequences of creating a metanarrative of coaching. The many 'little voices' Lyotard refers to reflects the diversity of practices and models which constitute coaching and which in turn reflects the diversity of individuals and organizations who seek the support of coaching. Peterson (2006) concurs and suggests that humans are complex and multifaceted, which is backed up by Garvey et al. (2009: 5), who suggest that 'one size does not fit all'. Peterson (2006: 51) concurs and states: '[t]herefore, behavioral approaches that reduce complex human behavior to mechanistic stimulus-and-response chains will not succeed'.

POWER WITHIN THE COACHING RELATIONSHIP

It is worth discussing the potential danger of an abuse of power within the coaching relationship, which could be exercised by either the client or the coachee. Both parties may attribute a position of power and authority to the coach due to their specialist knowledge. Alternatively, the client, especially if in a position of seniority, may feel the need to exert their authority over the coach in an attempt to intimidate or control them. Throughout his writings Michel Foucault warns against the seduction of power and suggests that the evils to be found in society have their roots in power. Recognizing the importance of power within the coaching relationship, Garvey et al. (2009) dedicate a whole chapter in their book to issues of power, suggesting that the power dynamics is a significant factor in the successful outcome of the coaching relationship. The power debate goes beyond the coaching relationship to encompass the power dynamics within the organization.

   This is a further example where the need for a coaching contract to be agreed between all parties from the outset is so important. The contract should clearly identify issues such as who the client is, the objectives to be achieved and how they will be achieved. This will go some way in eliminating the possibility of conflict between the objectives of the coachee and the objectives of the organization. The emphasis is on the coach to provide transparency about what it is they offer and, of equal importance, what they do not offer. There is a temptation on the part of the coach to try to be everything to everyone. Bachkirova and Kauffman (2009: 101) offer a warning against this and suggest that: '[t]he ambiguity of the term "coaching" should not be a good excuse for coaches to be vague and over-ambitious about what they can offer'.

It is inevitable that any new and emerging profession is likely to attract practitioners with a wide range of skills and abilities, from the novice to the master, and coaching is no exception. As Passmore and McGoldrick (2009) note, counselling is often seen as a proxy for coaching, and a cynic would suggest it is because coaching can demand a higher fee than that of counsel-ling. Furthermore, it is also much easier to provide coaching services than counselling since to practise as a coach does not yet require formal training or a qualification. The absence of a professional body tasked to regulate the profession means that training and development is also ad hoc, and just as the quality of coaching services varies, so does the availability and quality of training and development. Provision of programmes there-fore varies from one day to a two-year Masters degree and with different options in between. Brockbank and McGill (2006) express their concern over the quality of some of the training on offer and observe that: '[a] vast choice of training is on offer, as more providers enter the field, not always of high quality'. The bogus claims made by some providers confidently declare that their programmes guarantee participants a lucrative income. Equally disturbing are the attributes associated with specific dis-ciplines and promoted by their authors as being the 'holy grail' of coaching. Coaches and coachees alike would do well to heed the warning of Clutterbuck and Megginson (2011): '[t]he afi-cionados of these philosophies or disciplines are often highly enthusiastic, but this enthusiasm may at times hide a dangerous trap – the implicit assumption that this philosophy, powerful as it may be, is always the best approach for every client'.

As with any new and emerging profession, there are bound to be numerous communities of practice who will both influ-ence its practice and development, as well as claiming to be the most suitable in determining the identity of the profession. As Stewart et al. (2008) rightly point out, the absence of an agreed model makes it difficult to validate the claims made as to the outcomes and contributions attributed to coaching. Downey

(2003) offers an interesting observation that the effectiveness of coaching tends to be measured by the achievements of those being coached, which is not necessarily the only or most appropriate measure to determine the success or failure of coaching.

The term *evidence* traditionally associated with credible research presents its own challenges as different researchers would seek different forms of evidence in the same way as the word *truth* has different meanings and interpretations, depending on the particular philosophical position from which the researcher approaches their research. Moreover, as suggested earlier, coaching will mean different things to different people, with each coach influenced by their own experiences, education and biases resulting in a style most comfortable to them. As has also been eluded to earlier, a standardized approach to coaching is not necessarily the best solution, as it might be more appropriate and beneficial for the client if the coach adapts their style to meet the needs and circumstances of the coachee.

As will be discussed at length in Chapter 3, postmodernism strongly advocates diversity and the promotion of difference, and strongly contests the metanarratives associated with various institutions and the power and control they wield. I concur with the caution offered by Garvey (2011: 29) as follows: 'Definition would provide focus but it would also exclude.' Instead, I advocate the notion of little narratives as put forward by Lyotard and which I will discuss in greater depth in the following chapter. As an evolving profession, coaching would benefit from the scepticism of critical thinking and understand the consequences and implications of creating a metanarrative of coaching. In doing so the conclusion may be that the benefit of coaching is the fact that it has the flexibility to reflect the diversity of individuals and organizations seeking the support of coaching by responding with diverse practices and models and not succumbing to the illusion of a metanarrative.

CONCLUSION

Coaching has the potential to provide the same degree of development and change at the organizational level as it achieves at the individual level, and at the same time confront the assumptions and ideologies of organizations. However, as Garvey et al. (2009) point out, '[c]oaching and mentoring are essentially one-to-one practices and so those studying, researching and working in the area tend to ignore the wider, social and organizational implications of their work'. The roots of a humanistic philosophy are evident in the statement of Kemp (2008), who suggests that it is 'a human development methodology'. This reflects a fundamental core value of coaching evident in other caring professions, such as psychology, therapy and counselling, which means much of the coaching relationship is grounded on the support offered to the coachee. It is for this reason I suggest coaching that provides a more thought-provoking approach, such as one grounded in a critical perspective, may be better equipped to challenge organizations and their leaders to be more aware of their ideologies and assumptions. The following chapter introduces the fundamentals of critical theory and puts forward an argument for it as a philosophical foundation to coaching.

CRITICAL THEORY: A PHILOSOPHY OF COACHING

3

CHAPTER OBJECTIVES

- Introduce critical theory as a philosophy
- Discuss scepticism as a category of critical theory
- Describe groupthink as it applies to organizations
- Identify sceptical coaching and its value to coaching

INTRODUCTION

The reflections of Clutterbuck and Megginson (2011) suggest that although there is a need for the maintenance of standards in the emerging coaching profession, it is not possible to measure the diversity and creativity of coaching through 'simplistic classifications [which] are likely to be divisive and of dubious validity. What's needed is a conceptual framework that reflects the evolution of complexity in coaches' way of thinking about themselves, their clients and the context, in which they operate.' Small (2003) argues that the study of philosophy is particularly useful in a business environment which is underscored by uncertainty and because as coaches we work predominantly within a business context, this is of particular value to us as I will argue in this chapter. I would expect that the majority of business leaders and managers would perceive the study of philosophy to be totally detached from the day-to-day challenges they have to deal with. However, as Small (2003) argues, the literature on management would suggest that the way in which a manager carries out their various managerial duties is significantly influenced by their individual value system and the particular philosophy that directs their thinking. The assumption that philosophy has no bearing on management may be attributed to what we understand philosophy to be. It has historically been defined as the pursuit of knowledge and more recently it is also perceived as seeking an understanding of such knowledge. Small (2003: 84) divides philosophy into a number of sub-categories, namely:

1. metaphysics, ontology or the nature of existence and of coming to be;
2. epistemology or the study of the theory of knowledge;
3. moral philosophy and the origins and justification of moral codes; and
4. analysing issues such as justice, happiness, and right and wrong behaviour.

As Small (2003) points out, the sophists, predecessors to Socrates, as semi-professional teachers taught a great range of subjects, which included rhetoric, oratory, ethics, political theory, law, history, mnemonics, literature, mathematics, astronomy, metaphysics and epistemology, which had a significant influence on subjects we identify as politics, education, ethics and cultural studies and therefore by extension our understanding of management. I would suggest that these categories have a significant contribution to make to our understanding and practice of coaching. In order to build our knowledge and capacity to coach, we engage in the pursuit of the knowledge of coaching supported by the relevant underpinning theories. Our ethical stance to coaching is seen not only by clients and client organizations as important, but all professional bodies of coaching promote their own particular ethical principles which they expect their members to adhere to. I have no doubt that a study of Plato and his extensive writings on knowledge and justice would have had particular bearing on the behaviours of investors and executives of the banks whose gross misconduct contributed to the collapse of the banking sector. As Small (2003: 191) argues, people enter business for a number of reasons, such as making a profit and motivations of self-interest. Success in business depends on the ability of managers and business leaders to use their *nous*, which involves '[t]he intellect, and includes a measure of prudence, honesty and fairness'. Philosophy has a great deal to offer in developing the knowledge and understanding of these practices and in developing the integrity and ethical behaviour expected of business leaders.

I argue that the formal study of philosophy in management studies would greatly enhance the quality of thinking within organizations and the leadership of such institutes and as we as coaches practice our coaching within the context of an organization, we would similarly benefit from an increased understanding of the contribution of philosophy to our own practices. A philosophy of coaching allows the coach to reflect deeply on their personal ontological position in relation to the nature of truth and how they will therefore approach their coaching practice. Having a clearly defined philosophy provides a guiding framework through which the coach is able to engage in personal reflection as well as reflecting on the interactions and relationships with their clients. Having a personal philosophy that underpins and guides the particular stance of the coach, provides the coach with the means to transcend models, processes or discipline-specific coaching and to define their own unique position within the coaching dynamic. The starting point of developing a personal philosophy of coaching is for the coach to reflect on the meaning of truth and what truth means to them and their coaching practice. We can look at truth in the wider context as to how we view the world and our place within that world and for the purpose of putting the notion of truth in the context of coaching, it would inform our views on what we perceive to be true of coaching. In other words, we would reflect on what are the underlying principles of our coaching based on what we as individuals perceive coaching to be, what we want to achieve with our coaching, our relationship with our coachees, the ethical principles which we associate with our underlying philosophy, and so forth. Let us explore in more detail how we may define the elusive notion of truth.

THE NATURE OF TRUTH

There are broadly speaking two views on the nature of truth and reality, namely positivism and interpretivism (Easterby-Smith *et al.*, 1991). The position one adopts will determine the view one holds as to the nature of truth, human behaviour and what is defined as social reality. These two different perspectives are often perceived as being on opposite ends of a continuum. Simplistically put, positivism suggests that it is through observation that we can identify laws that govern the social world. Furthermore, these laws are transferable from one context to another; for example, the law of gravity or attraction. It also suggests that we arrive at knowledge by gathering so called 'facts' which then go on to provide the basis for these laws. It also suggests that this quest for discovering these facts and laws should be conducted in a value-free manner and therefore not influenced by the biases, assumptions or values of the individual seeker. This particular position of truth is also identified under different labels, including modernism, objectivism and rationalism. It seeks to understand the specific laws and facts associated with specific phenomena and I suggest that much of management and organizational practice and research have been approached from this particular viewpoint. In the previous chapter I discussed the two parallel paths the development of coaching seems to have taken, and the focus on techniques and models seems to be underpinned by positivism.

However, an alternative view is that an observer or researcher is not the clinical, detached observer science so painstakingly tries to achieve, but that the observer is part of the process of emergence. Interpretivism, on the other end of the continuum, therefore suggests that the world is too complex to be reduced to law-like generalizations. It is underpinned by a belief that knowledge can only become known from a personal or cultural-specific perspective and can therefore never become objective or universal. This viewpoint challenges the idea of reality being external to the individual and therefore the existence of an objective knowledge. Instead, Morgan and Smircich (1980) propose that knowledge is the product of social construction. The positivistic perspective emphasizes objectivity, distance and control and considers these as fundamental to the process of conducting *real* research (Denzin and Lincoln, 2000). However, Morgan (1983) argues that as a result of the interaction between observer and the object being observed, the object obtains its objectivity through the act of observation. Objectivity is therefore seen as a property originating from the observers. Other labels associated with this position are relativism, idealism, postmodernism and perspectivism.

If we apply the ideas of interpretivism to organizations, organizational activities are then sustained through negotiations and interpretations by a group of individuals and in the process of understanding their organization which the researcher needs to take into account when attempting to determine any truths associated with the organization. An organization therefore has to be understood from the multiple meaning systems beyond the single individual and the competing views of what constitutes organizational reality. I will discuss the ideas of constructionism at length in a later chapter, but briefly it suggests that organizational activities are sustained through negotiations and interpretations by a group of individuals. In an attempt to understand organizations, the researcher (or coach in this context) needs to consider these group activities and processes when seeking the truth about an organization and those within it. An organization has to be understood from the multiple meaning systems beyond the single individual and the competing views of what constitutes organizational reality. It is therefore much more complex and more messy than would be suggested from the perspective of positivism.

To reach the level of maturity suggested by Clutterbuck and Megginson (2011) I investigate and discuss how interpretivism can support the coach in developing a deeper understanding of the philosophy that underpins their practice. Denzin and Lincoln (2000) propose that interpretivism is synonymous with constructionism with a shared goal of understanding the complex world of lived experiences from the perspective of the individual. Furthermore, what is relevant to an exploration and understanding of coaching is the assumption that knowledge is perceived as being constructed relationally. The interpretivist view also accepts that multiple views therefore coexist within the meaning we impose on various experiences rather than meaning existing independently in the world and outside our experiences of it. Different people will experience the same situation differently, influenced by their own unique experiences, cultural backgrounds, personal values and beliefs – their own unique set of filters. Human relationships and human actions are infused by intentions, values and beliefs and as coaches we know that relationships are at the heart of coaching. If we are therefore to understand human action we need to understand the internal logic that drives such action. Gergen (1997), a key proponent of constructionism, suggests that the world gets constructed through the engagement and discussions between people when they interact with each other relationally. I will return to a discussion of constructionism in subsequent chapters as it is a significant part of the coaching relationship and what I perceive as the *black box* of coaching. I want to continue with the discussion of a philosophy of coaching by introducing the concept of postmodernism as it embraces a perspective associated with the interpretivist paradigm, namely that of critical theory, and a specific aspect of critical theory, namely scepticism. It will become clear as the chapter unfolds as to why I have focused on this particular philosophical stance as an example of how philosophy can inform the practice of the coach.

POSTMODERNISM

What is postmodernism and why are we interested in understanding what postmodernism can add to the notion of truth? I argue that it has a great deal to say about truth and how that may underpin our practice of coaching. We think of the French philosopher Lyotard as the father of postmodernism. He first and foremost encourages a scepticism towards the motives of various institutional authorities and what he has defined as their metanarratives. Metanarratives, or grand narratives, are defined as large-scale theories and philosophies of the world. Lyotard is deeply suspicious of these and argues that narratives of this kind are inadequate in representing the truth about society and its complexities. Instead, Lyotard argues for diversity and what he has come to term difference and an abundance of little narratives or versions of truth as opposed to one grand narrative at the exclusion of other perspectives. Lyotard goes on to argue strongly that the domination of the ideology of a metanarrative leads to the suppression of other ideologies or different perspectives as to the nature of truth. In his most famous work, *The Postmodern Condition* (1979), Lyotard argues for the replacement of grand narratives and their accompanied assumptions of prediction and control. Lyotard suggests that a postmodernist society functions on a high level of abstraction and uncertainty, a belief shared by constructionism and which I will discuss in a later chapter.

Lyotard suggests that little narratives come into being through the interaction of a group for a specific reason and at a particular moment in time, which by their nature accept difference and the transient nature of knowing. A postmodernist knowledge of everyday life therefore invites a multitude of alternative voices to contribute different views and perspectives on what is perceived as truth. What is important is not therefore whether these little narratives are true or false, but that they serve a purpose at a given time. Lyotard argues that society is complex and filled with uncertainties that require the creativity of little narratives to deal with it, and grand narratives aim to repress individual creativity for the purpose of protecting a particular grand narrative. In essence grand narratives are perceived as the oppressive force of authoritarianism. Truth from a postmodern perspective is therefore fluid and ever changing and the most that is to be hoped for is a snapshot at a particular moment in time.

Lyotard also suggests that as societies we have ceased to believe in the grand narratives of large-scale theories and philosophies as to what constitutes truth. Instead, we are much more open to difference and diversity, which has resulted in the little narratives that represent his postmodernist ideas. The little narrative proposed by Lyotard is seen as the antithesis of the grand narrative; it represents flexibility and constantly reinvents itself, which liberates it from the weight of tradition and the restrictions of preconceived ideologies. Lyotard argues passionately that grand narratives are nothing less than mechanisms with which to suppress the individual. So, instead, the little narrative emerges to meet the needs of a particular situation without any reference to larger and dominant philosophy.

Coaching, as an emerging profession, clearly has groups vying for the opportunity to influence and own what would become the metanarrative of coaching. Such a metanarrative would dictate and determine who practises coaching, in what way, using which techniques and the training and development the coach should receive to practise coaching, etc. On the other hand, the argument for little narratives as proposed by postmodernist thinkers suggests that individuals in society need to make their little narratives heard and to challenge the metanarratives imposed on them by those in authority. In conclusion the theme throughout this text, supported by various theorists, concurs with the central tenet of postmodernism which suggests that the equivocal postmodern world is permeated with different interpretations and conflicting interests, and is populated by people with multiple and ever-changing identities. I now turn the attention to scepticism to further discuss the postmodern argument's potential contribution to a coaching philosophy.

CRITICAL THEORY AND SCEPTICISM

As I have discussed in Chapter 2, the evidence and theoretical basis of coaching is tenuous and sparse (Jones, 2012). At the heart of the philosophy of research is scepticism and either the acceptance or rejection of various hypothesis put forward. The role of the researcher is therefore to ask challenging questions for the purpose of getting closer to what constitutes truth of a particular discourse. Scepticism is not synonymous with cynicism, but its purpose is to be challenging the prevailing discourse so that the boundaries of our knowledge about the particular subject can be expanded through new and deeper insight as to what constitutes truth associated with the subject, such as coaching for example. Critical theorists strongly challenge the notion that a definitive description of 'truth' and 'reality' exists independent of our experiences and perceive these concepts to be interpreted and understood within a social context. Critical theory builds on the human legacy of our ability to doubt and question established customs and ideologies and in particular the institutions that produce the ideologies in the first place, as outlined in the discussion on postmodernism above.

The roots of critical theory can be traced back to the Enlightenment, when some key thinkers began to challenge the dogmas associated with religion. Their tradition of critical theory supports our ability to have a questioning attitude towards the claims of truth offered by those in power and the institutions they represent. However, it is worth pointing out at the outset that critical theory does not have a monopoly on truth nor does it represent an alternative ideology (du Toit and Sim, 2010). Instead it is an invitation to engage in debate for the purpose of critical self-reflection and to understand how communication becomes distorted due to the processes of power (McAuley et al., 2006). It is therefore one possible version of truth rather than *the* version of truth. I suggest that much of organizational parlance reflects a language which, when challenged, appears to lack substance and meaning. Critical theory sets out to challenge a number of aspects of organizations, such as the dominant language and terms of reference that reflect values such as toughness, competition and a plethora of associations with sport metaphors. We also observe how the roles and titles assigned to individuals become fixed and may become an identity straitjacket and an issue that often surfaces within a coaching context.

Critical theory is a broad church and includes the virtues of scepticism, which encourages radical and ongoing assessment of belief systems and their perceived wisdoms. It is particularly aimed at challenging dominant ideologies. Garvey (2011: 31) concurs and suggests that: 'The dominant language tends to be one that holds sway, it is the power position.' The value of scepticism to a coaching approach is the concept of balancing both support and challenge offered to the coachee. As we saw earlier, postmodernism shares the scepticism critical theory has of the perceived homogeneity subscribed to by those in power and instead argues that the world around us is characterized by difference. In fact, the value of difference and different definitions are that it creates different narratives which results in different discourses leading to different practices and flexibility to meet the differing needs people have. Postmodernism sets out to undermine the grand narratives of our culture and Jean-François Lyotard in particular encouraged the rejection of institutional authority which he suggests invariably includes the suppression of divergent points of view. I therefore suggest that critical theory offers a framework for coaching which allows the coach to challenge the power structures found within organizational environments. Furthermore, critical theory is rich in concepts that enable us to construct new narratives of coaching, thereby furthering the debate and understanding as to what constitutes coaching.

A coaching practice influenced by scepticism would have gone a long way towards challenging the fundamentalist ideologies that had created so many problems in the business world at the time of writing (du Toit and Sim, 2010). One of the key values of coaching is that it is a powerful mechanism through which to assist the individual in addressing both their own internal barriers as well as the powerful barriers that exist within organizations. Coaching is the process through which we are able to challenge the stories and narratives that come to dominate not only an organization but also the behaviours of those within it. To assist the coach in developing a sceptical or questioning attitude, there is a rich tradition of thought in philosophy to draw on, including contemporary postmodernism, which is committed to the scrutiny of authority, its assumptions and practices. Such a perspective encourages the coachee to examine their own beliefs with a view to see what lies behind them and to question whether they are more than tradition or habit. Applying the principles of scepticism allows the coach to ask the awkward questions that help the coachee to foster an enquiring mind at all times.

As suggested above, Lyotard (1979) sets forth a general argument against grand narratives, or metanarratives, he argues that these had lost their credibility by the later 20th century and ought to be subjected to sustained challenge to undermine the power they wielded. What was wanted then, in his view, was for an attitude of 'incredulity toward metanarratives' to be fostered. The way forward was to be 'little narratives' instead, which were not committed to any overall theory of everything, as in the manner of Marxism or capitalism, and were, as Lyotard saw it, responsive to the uniqueness of 'events' as they unfolded in time. As Lyotard argues, the intention of grand narratives is to predetermine events, which for Lyotard was impossible and supported by the arguments put forward by constructionism and sensemaking, to be discussed in future chapters. Little narratives may be associated with pressure groups who assemble to stand in opposition to the perceived abuses of institutionalized power. The caveat, of course, is that the movement dissolves once the particular abuse is neutralized to avoid the temptation for the movement to grow into a grand narrative of its own and impose its will on others in the time-honoured fashion. Postmodernism is particularly suspicious of the creation of power blocs as it perceives these as being the suppressors of difference in our culture.

History suggests that the temptation to those in power is to refuse, acknowledge or accept the validity of different views and, furthermore, they are predisposed to settle disputes on the basis of their own set of values. The role of little narratives was there-fore to address the imbalance and to create the space for dissent-ing voices to be heard, thereby holding the dominant ideology to account. Lyotard vehemently opposed what he perceived as the totalizing tendency of grand narratives, which set out to impose their worldview on others. The purpose of postmodern thought from the outset was to position itself in opposition to authority and it has been at the forefront of challenging the assumptions associated with institutional power. Assuming the broad-based approach of postmodernism as a general cultural trend as opposed to being a specific movement, it is possible to see the value it offers in the nurturing of an attitude of suspicion towards grand narratives. The benefit of a more sceptical approach in public life would be a very positive development as grand narra-tives deserve to be challenged and questioned wherever they are to be found. All institutions, not only those of a political leaning and including organizations, have their own grand narrative, which is often imposed on others and defended by senior man-agement against internal and external criticism. As with any grand narratives, the purpose is to ensure compliance with its principles and practices at both the individual as well as group level. Not only is conformity seen as a virtue by those controlling the grand narrative, but subscribing to the particular grand nar-rative is also rewarded. Challenge is seen as a barrier to progress rather than as a catalyst for innovation and reinvention.

Instead, postmodernism provides a framework through which we are first of all able to recognize oppressive narratives where they present themselves and then to mount a challenge in favour of a plurality of narratives as a much more inclusive approach. Narrative in itself is a universal phenomenon, intrinsic to human communication, and as we will see in following chapters, intimately associated with coaching. However, in the opinion of postmodernism, put forward by Lyotard, the problem is when we collude with certain narratives allowing them to become the voices of authority, establishing a power base that rejects alternative voices. Narrative plays a fundamental role in our social existence; without it our societies will be unable to function. The problem that often arises, however, is that narratives become legitimated by reference to an outside authority, resulting in certain narratives being seen as representing the 'truth'. Lyotard throws down the gauntlet and challenges us instead to cultivate a pragmatic attitude towards narrative, judging it on its social utility rather than slavishly and blindly adhering to a specific set of principles. He also campaigned for a plurality of narratives with a constant stream of little narratives to invigorate debates allowing for different views and thereby preventing the stagnation of ideas.

The necessity of narrative is to be defended; however, the grand narrative is to be resisted at all costs. It is worth pointing out that scepticism does not oppose strong beliefs, but instead it provides a constant check to ensure those opinions do not put themselves forward as the bearer of a grand narrative. This position allows one to be constantly engaged in dialogue with the opinions of others, facilitating debates through which our understanding and knowledge is expanded. In summary, critical theory is the scrutiny of institutions and practices and the ideologies they produce (Alvesson and Willmott, 1996). It seeks to advance and nurture the human potential and to critically oppose and question the practices of institutions and those in power who seek to marginalize or suppress this ideal.

CRITICAL THEORY AND ORGANIZATIONS

The application of critical theory to social sciences, which includes the theories of organizations, is largely attributed to the Frankfurt School. Established in the 1920s, its mission was fundamentally to question the assumptions of the social sciences, which suggested they had the capability to produce value-free knowledge of social reality. Germany in the early 1930s provided numerous institutions and ideologies that systematically oppressed the autonomy of society. The institutions of power referred to above include organizations, and the claims of so-called management experts and critical theory entered the debate on organizational theory in the late 1980s (McAuley et al., 2006). McAuley et al. (2006) go on to propose that at the centre of critical theory in organizations is the proposition that the way they are structured discourages fundamental questioning about the very nature of organizations. So many of the assumptions underlying management, leadership, the role of organizations, to name a few, are taken for granted and go unchallenged. Critical management theory seeks to question the often unnoticed practices within organizations that favour some individuals or groups at the expense of others. The consequences of these organizational practices are that they are rarely scrutinized or contested nor are they held to account. The result is often injustices, not only within organizations, but in society at large. As Voronov (2008) points out, traditional or mainstream researchers often err on the side of management without taking into account the perspectives of or impact on other, often less powerful, stakeholders.

The purpose of critical theory in organizations is therefore to challenge and question the organizational values and practices that are revered and have a sense of normality. One example is the lack of diversity at the more senior levels of organizations with alternative values and practices, such as feminism, often being marginalized. The value of critical theory in organizations is that it fosters reflective practices that allow its members to become less entranced by the perceived inevitability of the organizational ideals and the manipulation of charismatic corporate leaders (Alvesson and Willmott, 1996). Management wisdom is often shrouded in neutrality, and supported by scientific reason and devoid of any moral commitments. However, the perceived rationality of management decisions often has a devastating impact on individuals and societies, and yet they are excluded from the decision-making process. Through the emancipatory power of critical theory the received wisdoms of management practices are scrutinized whilst seeking to find alternative values and practices that are more beneficial to all stakeholders of the organization. The outcome will be that decisions are the result of democratic choice rather than the outcome of a small group of elite in positions of power whose reasoning and beliefs go unchallenged.

However, the critical spirit of scepticism is often endangered through suppression or dilution. The most poignant reminder of the need for critical self-reflection and the vigilance against the temptation of a grand narrative has to be represented by the experience of the financial collapse of recent years (du Toit and Sim, 2010). The sector is an example of what can happen when an institution becomes resistant to criticism – how the mighty may fall. Any system needs sceptical voices offering differing views no matter how unsettling they may appear, for the purpose of making us think and thereby avoiding a collapse of the scale witnessed in the financial sector. The ripples of the collapse of these institutions continue to impose devastating effects on countries and their economies around the world and the day-to-day lives of the ordinary citizens of those countries. As Sim (2004) suggests, there is a tendency for dogmatism to emerge as power structures are created. As the critical theorist Michel Foucault (2006) admonishes, power is very seductive and those who gain it rarely relinquish it easily. Instead, Foucault argues that power is the source of most of the evils that beset our cultures; whether it is to be found within the corridors of political institutions or organizational board rooms, power opposes any challenges aimed at eroding its position of control. As organizations do not have a system of opposition that forms part of the political system, it may therefore be even more resistant to the need for change and the inclusion of different points of view.

A challenge levied against critical management theory is that journals tend to favour researchers of academic research and fail to give voice to knowledge generated by practitioners (Voronov, 2008). This makes critical management scholars guilty of the very weaknesses they oppose. Voronov (2008) goes on to throw down the gauntlet to critical management theorists and proposes that they embrace the world of practice and learn to discover new ways of contributing to the field.

That is precisely what I propose in the following section: combining the practice with the theory for the purpose of applying critical theory to the practice of coaching.

SCEPTICAL COACHING

Turning the ideas of Lyotard to the context within which coaching is often employed, namely that of organizations, it offers coaching the framework through which to challenge the organizational grand narratives and expose them to scrutiny. Furthermore, the value to the emerging profession of coaching offered by the scepticism associated with postmodernism is the awareness of the seduction of a grand narrative of coaching represented by the range of disciplines, models and techniques all claiming to represent the 'truth' of coaching. Instead, a pick' n mix approach that draws on the many different tools has the flexibility of meeting the needs of individual coaching circumstances. The whole body of coaching therefore offers a spectrum of methods that can be raided for deployment in making sense of the situation presented. Critical theory offers a rich vein of theoretical concepts that allows those with an open mind to gain new perspectives on situations and to construct new narratives that will not only further the debate of coaching, but also benefit the recipients of the practice (du Toit and Sim, 2010).

Postmodernist thinkers like Jean-François Lyotard have a lot to offer the emerging coaching profession, not only through their scepticism of what we think we know, but also what we can ever hope to know. As is evidenced by the scientific community, which instead of producing knowledge and certainty continually reveals the mysteries of the unknown which science seems incapable of resolving. The result is that the utopia of a theory of everything seems to be an elusive dream and it might be that there are things we could never know or even have the ability to know. The Grand Unified Theory (GUT) remains an enigma to the scientific community, despite the sporadic claims that we are on the verge of it. In fact, there are those within the scientific community who are beginning to question whether a total understanding of the physical realm is in fact possible.

Ultimately, scepticism can be defined as a state of mind more than anything else, accompanied by the willingness to challenge and be challenged. Coaching as an emerging discourse has much to gain en route to maturity as a profession, benefiting from the richness and the inclusion many little narratives have to offer. Although uncomfortable to some and offering many challenges to the notion of regulation, an inclusive approach to coaching will continue to provide challenge to existing practices and assumptions whilst offering different perspectives to the coaching approach both academically as well as practically. It also reflects the complexity and variety of scenarios presented to the coaching situation. Scepticism is a very powerful tool in the toolbox of the coach in challenging the received wisdoms it may encounter whether represented by the coachee or the organizational context. In fact, we could argue that coaching has much in common with scepticism as both set out to question everyday beliefs and associated assumptions. The role of the coach is to challenge traditions and the validity and existence of disempowering values and beliefs. As discussed elsewhere, a valuable lesson offered by the theories of complex adaptive systems is that a system needs to be kept on the edge of chaos to avoid entropy. As we argue (du Toit and Sim, 2010), scepticism is central to any healthy system as it provides a counter-balance to the temptation of dogma. However, as we also suggest, scepticism has its own drawbacks. It is undeniably perceived as negative and possibly fault-finding in its approach. It is worth pointing out that it is a technique that I have argued is of benefit to coaching rather than promoting it as an ideology in its own right.

So why then should we associate scepticism with coaching? As I argued above, scepticism has great practical as well as philosophical value to our daily existence, including the context within which coaching takes place. I am not suggesting scepticism for the sake of it, but as an attitude through which to challenge authority whether it is in the shape of an organization or the belief system of a coachee. As seen in the previous chapter, numerous proponents of coaching suggest that a successful outcome of coaching is for the coachee to be able to self-coach once the coaching relationship has come to an end. The benefit of a sceptical awareness is therefore to provide the coachee with the ability to offer healthy scrutiny to not only their own but also the organization's beliefs and behaviours thereby avoiding destructive dogmatism from taking hold. A further benefit is for the coachee to engage in critical self-reflection on their role of collusion in keeping potentially oppressive ideologies and practices alive within their organizations.

DISTORTED GROUPTHINK

We were first alerted to the dangers of groupthink by Janis in the 1970s, identifying it as a phenomenon that has had devastating effects not only on organizations but which has also resulted in unnecessary loss of life due to flawed decisions taken during battle (the charge of the Light Brigade being one such example). The result of groupthink is a lack of self-censoring and the ability to think critically, leading to an insulation of the group from others within the organization or the wider society. The shared illusion of a psychological safety within the group may result in erecting barriers against the need for change. Others external to the group may collude with them and turn a blind eye to group behaviours whilst they continue to perform and deliver results. However, if left unchecked a sense of invulnerability may grow and develop, which could result in deficient decision-making as a result of distorted thinking. Janis (1982) attributes the blind-spots identified with groupthink to inadequacies in information-processing. These inadequacies may lead to flawed decision-making, which is compounded over a period of time. Furthermore, the history of organizations would suggest that they fail to learn from the mistakes of the past.

The sense of solidarity and positive emotions associated with groupthink leads to a group cohesiveness which may in turn reject external challenge or criticism. There is also a tendency for the group to fall victim to significant errors, which further results in shared misjudgements. If discovered, the inclination is then to suppress or cover up information to disguise anomalies, and voices of dissent are silenced by imposing constraints on group members. This prevents public expression of doubt or challenge to group decisions and practices. Perceived deviants are isolated and possibly ostracized from the group if they persist in their challenge of the group. In fact, research has shown that the greater the group cohesiveness the greater is the likelihood of it rejecting nonconformists. The rejection is not only from within the ranks of the group, but also includes a rejection of outside critics who may threaten or challenge the status quo or group norms. As Janis (1972) asserts, the illusion of invulnerability contributes to a denial of possible inadequacies within the group, which may also limit the ability of the group to seek solutions to problems during a crisis.

Critical thinking has the ability to counteract the influence of groupthink by offering a healthy scepticism and a challenge to the assumptions of distorted thinking. As we discovered in our research of the demise of certain banks in the recent financial crisis, the power of groupthink is reliant on the compliance of everyone in the organization (du Toit and Sim, 2010). Influencing the changes referred to occurs once individuals within the group realize their contribution in maintaining the status quo, accepting that they are co-creators of the situation rather than the victim. It is within the culture of groupthink described above that coaching may act as a powerful intervention that could successfully challenge the group norms and the reality constructed within a particular organization or industry. Coaching being concerned with developing the individual and their faculty of self-awareness, places it in opposition to the groupthink mode. Furthermore, coaching has the potential to establish the practice of critical reflection with which to challenge the metanarrative of the organization.

As discussed in the previous chapter, coaching is particularly powerful in challenging internal and external barriers due to the fact that it addresses the values and beliefs individuals hold about the world, themselves and their place in the world. It is through narratives and the relaying of stories that organizational members communicate abstract ideas that create shared expectations and interpretations, thereby establishing group norms and patterns of behaviour. Shared beliefs result in shared habits which have the tendency to pave the way to ideologies that may go unquestioned. Coaching accompanied by scepticism has the ability to lead us away from uncritical beliefs and an acceptance of the status quo, which fosters an enquiring mind. The goal of critical coaching is therefore to encourage flexibility by responding to changing circumstances with a willingness to explore new avenues and ways of doing things without being constrained by dogmatic beliefs.

Radical coaching as a product of a sceptical mindset associated with critical theory has the potential to counter the effects of groupthink. The likely self-development resulting from such an approach to coaching will naturally develop an independence of spirit in the coachee, encouraging them to see beyond the metanarrative and the possible destructive constraints of groupthink. Sceptical coaching will keep the awareness alive that different interpretations are always possible and act as an antidote to the risk of falling victim to blinkered traditions or conventions. The lesson for coaches is to continually challenge their own beliefs and practices to guard against becoming the prisoner of specific frameworks resulting in a metanarrative of coaching which may very well exclude different perspectives. As Garvey (2011: 23) so eloquently puts it: 'While a consensus offers clarity for the majority, it can disempower or downgrade the minority as the majority view holds sway.' The idea of challenging a metanarrative of coaching is supported by Garvey (2011: 18), who suggests that: 'coaching and mentoring activities are socially constructed, dynamic and subject to reconstruction in various settings to suit a variety of purposes'. The challenges Foucault levies at the institutions who exercise their power over the majority are worthy of consideration. These considerations should inform the debates whether to support the professionalization of coaching and the establishing of a professional body, and the possibility of creating an elitist group who make the decision as to what does and doesn't constitute coaching. In order to make coaching more transparent and less associated with specific models or techniques, I explore in the following chapters the elements of the black box of coaching as alluded to in the introduction.

CONCLUSION

In this chapter I have drawn on the underlying principles of critical theory and scepticism as a philosophical position within the overarching perspective of postmodernism. It is one example of how a philosophical perspective can underpin and support a stance to the practice of coaching. Furthermore, having an underlying philosophy of coaching does not preclude any of the models or techniques associated with different practices. Instead, as the perspective of little narratives would suggest, the coach has the opportunity to populate their coaching toolbox with any of the many techniques and models they consider to be supportive of their philosophical approach. One then becomes the eclectic coach Clutterbuck and Megginson (2011) referred to. Furthermore, I also suggest that the particular ideology of postmodernism will prevent the emerging coaching profession from inadvertently creating a metanarrative of coaching which will be in danger of excluding the richness of diversity and creativity currently marking the practice of coaching.

THE PREREQUISITES OF COACHING

4

CHAPTER OBJECTIVES

- The importance of contracting with all key stakeholders
- Establishing the coaching relationship and the willingness of the coachee to be coached
- Building trust and the psychological contract
- The nature of the coaching space and the influence of the presence of the coach

INTRODUCTION

Having discussed what I believe to be the most important consideration for the coach, namely that of the philosophical underpinning of their coaching practice, we can now turn our attention to addressing the prerequisites of coaching. The success of coaching does not happen by chance and the coach needs to pay attention to a number of factors in establishing the conditions that will facilitate a successful and rewarding relationship. The path to being a successful coach includes many aspects other than the mastery of coaching itself. It requires the ability to build the relationship with the coachee, organization and other stakeholders, engage in continuous personal development for the purpose of drawing on multiple theoretical and practical perspectives, inhabit the complex and ambiguous environment of their clients and deal with the dynamic and changing landscape of the coaching context. I will discuss in this chapter what I perceive as some of the prerequisites to coaching.

CONTRACTING

Kahn (2011) suggests that from the outset of the coaching relationship the coach must successfully integrate and align the needs and expectations of the sponsoring organization. The perceived success of coaching will mean different things to different people, depending on their perception of value. As Moen and Federici (2012) point out, achievement-oriented environments driven by competition and performance focus on tangible and objective measures, which would suggest that their measure of the success of coaching would be based on maximizing individual performance and financial returns. Therefore, the purpose of contracting before embarking on coaching with a client will determine the measures of success as well as establishing clear commitments between the coach, coachee and the organization, often represented by the line manager. The contract will provide clarity on specific issues such as scheduling, procedures for rearranging appointments, objectives and expected outcomes of the coaching contract. The question of who is the client, the coachee, or buyer of the coaching intervention, such as the organization, may oftentimes lead to a dilemma for the coach and possible conflicting loyalties in determining who is the client in the coaching relationship.

A further important consideration as part of the contracting process is to clearly identify how feedback will be provided to the sponsor and by whom. Coupled with the last point is determining how records of the coaching sessions will be kept, if at all, and whose responsibility it will be. Kahn (2011) suggests that the most important consideration of the coaching relationship is that of its relatedness, which includes a relationship with the organizational context and culture. Awareness of the psychological contract during the contracting stage extends to include the context and relationships the coachee is engaged in, such as a relationship with their line manager, peers and subordinates. This is to include the expectations of the line manager, their possible involvement and support provided. Doing so as part of the contracting stage will avoid possible misunderstandings at a later stage.

As the coaching market matures, there are increasing requirements on the emerging profession. For example, coaches are expected to demonstrate engagement in formal qualifications and to have gained increasingly higher coaching qualifications (Whitmore, 2011). In addition, they also need to provide evidence of ongoing CPD activities. As part of the contracting stage, the coach needs to demonstrate not only their competencies and skills of coaching, but also their particular approach to coaching. This aspect returns to what I consider as one of the most important elements of the development of the coach, namely to identify the philosophy that underpins and drives their coaching. Having addressed this question for themselves, the coach will be in a stronger position to articulate the nature of their coaching approach. According to Drake (2011), any notion of master development requires a path in which the coach grows not only in their technical proficiency but also in their personal and relational maturation for the purpose of being able to deal with the increased complexity of the environment in which their clients operate. Drake (2011: 146) summarizes the continual development of the coach across four domains of knowledge, which enhances (1) their *awareness* of their internal states, the client, the conversation and the environment, (2) what they need to pay *attention* to, (3) their ability to *adapt* and (4) their *accountability* for their practice and its consequences. His interpretation of mastery resonates with the systemic eclectic coach as put forward by Clutterbuck and Megginson (2011). It suggests that the master coach has a wider field of awareness, which includes a confidence in their own abilities, experience of the field and what to focus their attention on. Their experience also allows them to identify patterns that require them to adapt their approach to meet the needs of the client.

The coaching profession is also under increased pressure to demonstrate the value of their intervention to the organization, and in particular the return on investment. As a coach, you may very well find yourself in a position during the contracting stage of having to defend the perceived contribution coaching is likely to deliver in relation to the financial investment by the organization. Throughout this text I challenge whether this is a relevant or even possible measure of coaching and whether it actually does it justice. This challenge is supported by Grant (2012), who argues that it is not only unreliable, but that an exclusive focus on financial measures result in the exclusion of the extensive range of positive outcomes achieved through coaching. Given that a financial measurement of the success of a coaching outcome is both limited and unreliable, Grant (2012) suggests that the focus needs to be on two important variables instead, namely workplace engagement and wellbeing. As he argues, organizations function much more effectively when their employees demonstrate facets of psychological wellbeing such as self-acceptance, purpose and positive relationships with others, all leading to their ability to engage in their work activities. Although a crucial reason for the existence of an organization, making money is not their sole purpose. They also provide a psychological context within which people work, relate, grow and develop which ultimately benefit the financial health of the organization. As Grant (2012: 82) argues, 'With coaching being able to deliver such a rich array of potential human benefits, financial ROI is indeed a poor and impoverished measure of coaching success.'

SUPERVISION

Increasingly when inviting potential coaches to respond to the tendering process, as is one of the preferred methods of recruiting coaches, organizations are also insistent on sight of how and when the coach engages in supervision. Engaging in supervision is not a 'nice to have', but a personal and business necessity. Coaching supervision is pivotal in the ongoing development of the professional coach and providing the challenge and support the coach needs in raising their self-awareness and awareness of their practice. In my experience there appears to be an implicit assumption among newly qualified coaches that once they have completed their chosen programme of study that further development and supervision is no longer a focus of attention. However, neglecting their development through regular supervision places them at a significant disadvantage to others who can provide evidence of ongoing supervision. It may very well be that the term 'supervision' is off-putting due to possible negative assumptions and images of control, monitoring and judgement associated with the term, particularly for coaches from a business background.

The coach who can demonstrate and provide evidence of regular supervision has the competitive edge when tendering or competing for coaching assignments. Anecdotal evidence would suggest that when a coach is in the early stages of developing their practice, the tendency is to save money by not engaging in supervision and limiting opportunities for ongoing CPD. In my experience in the economic climate at the time of writing, the ability of coaches to demonstrate their engagement in structured supervision and thereby providing quality assurance to prospective client organizations is paramount in securing a future as a professional coach.

Not only does supervision provide an individual coach with professional development, it also offers opportunities for reflective learning. There is no doubt that should the profession become regulated, supervision will be a requirement to practise. Other caring professions such as psychology, counselling and therapy have historically had supervision as part of their practice and ongoing development. Supervision is a formal process that can be pursued either on a one-to-one basis, in a group or a combination of both. Peer supervision facilitated by an experienced coach allows participants to learn from each other and to explore what works and what does not. Both approaches allow the coach to consciously spend time on developing their practice and their particular brand of coaching.

Unless an individual coach is part of an organization or a group of associates, it can be lonely and there comes a time in the career of any coach when they may be uncertain as to how effective they may be in meeting the needs of their clients. One of the greatest gifts we can leave our clients with is the ability to self-coach. Equally, in the same manner supervision provides the coach with the ability to develop the internal supervisor. It also provides the coach with the opportunity to learn about themselves as well as their practice.

The purpose of supervision is therefore to provide the coach with an environment in which the coach is able to reflect on their practice and for the resultant learning to inform their ongoing development and coaching approach. Just as it is important for a client to determine the quality and experience offered by a coach, so it is necessary for the coach to select a qualified and well-experienced supervisor. In order for the coach to gain benefit from the supervision, it has to take place regularly so that the breadth and depth of the coaching practice and framework can be reviewed and developed. A further significant benefit of supervision is the identification of themes and patterns for organizational learning without compromising the confidentiality of individual coachees. Supervision also provides assurance to the organization that any unethical or poor coaching is identified and improved upon. The supervisory approach scrutinizes the practice of the coach and identifies ways in which they can best meet the needs of their client and the organization.

Any coach, no matter how experienced, will at some stage in their practice find a client and/or situation challenging for many reasons. Within the supportive environment provided by supervision, the coach is able to analyse possible reasons and the ways in which to resolve the dissonance. A coaching client is always part of a wider system and associated complexities that surround their various relationships and roles. The supervisor is a valuable and impartial support to the coach in identifying the dynamics and the influence on the client and how the client presents these during the coaching sessions. Complex ethical dilemmas also form part of the milieu of coaching and the impartial perspective of the supervisor provides support in understanding the complexity and sensitivity surrounding such situations.

COACHING RELATIONSHIP

As we will see from the discussions of sensemaking in Chapter 5, meaning is dependent on relationships that are sustained through a common language that enables shared meaning to be created. In a coaching context, the quality of the sensemaking process appears to be reliant on the quality of the relationship between the coach and coachee. Numerous proponents of coaching support the importance of the relationship and Lenhardt (2004) suggests that it is within the alchemy created between the coach and coachee that the solutions and answers emerge to the questions of the coachee. As we have seen in Chapter 2, the discourses of psychology, counselling and therapy have made a significant contribution to coaching, and

O'Broin and Palmer (2007) draw a similarity with the therapeutic relationship. It suggests that the maintenance of trust is one of the important factors in creating the quality of the relationship. It is seen as a truism that the successful outcome of any coaching intervention is dependent on the quality of the relationship between the coach and the coachee (Fillery-Travis and Lane, 2007; Mäthner et al., 2005; O'Broin and Palmer, 2007). Despite the recognition of the importance of the relationship and its contribution to a successful coaching experience, O'Broin and Palmer (2007) suggest there is very little research available on the subject. The special nature of the relationship as experienced by one coachee is described as follows:

VIGNETTE

The special nature of the relationship between you and your coach is often marked by unique shared moments. It is not intimate, but it is a very special relationship which is identified by those shared moments that potentially could not be understood nor shared by others. I think it is true to say that you will probably never have the conversations with anyone else that you have with your coach, yet your coach is a stranger and you know that you may never see that person again after the conclusion of the coaching intervention. However, it is so special for that period of time. You would talk about and reflect on things and reveal things that you would never reveal to anyone else.

As the above vignette suggests, it is like no other relationship and described in a similar manner by Whitworth et al. (1998). The participants and data reinforce the claims by numerous proponents as to the nature of the relationship being influential in the quality of the experience (Fillery-Travis and Lane, 2007; Mäthner et al., 2005; O'Broin and Palmer, 2007). Irrespective of the coaching approach, one would concur with the view of Whitworth et al. (1998), who describe the coaching relationship as being unique. They go on to suggest that the ideal state for the coach to assume is to strive to be without judgement and accepting the coachee exactly for what they are. Unlike other methods of intervention, coaching aspires to resist the temptation to tell people what to do. Instead it is concerned with assisting and facilitating people in their sensemaking activities, supporting them in realizing their potential and removing the blocks that may be preventing them from doing so.

Furthermore, as I discuss on numerous occasions, the essence of coaching is to support the coachee to take ownership and responsibility for their attitudes, behaviours and circumstances. As Whitmore (2011) suggests, the overarching philosophy of the Big Society as promulgated by the UK Coalition government in power at the time of writing reflects the principle that we all need to take more responsibility for ourselves and the communities in which we live and interact. Whitmore (2011) goes on to say that it is part of an emerging global trend of moving away from hierarchical structures to increased self-responsibility observable in most cultures around the world. Furthermore, he proposes that the underlying principle of self-responsibility is needed everywhere: schools, universities, businesses, prisons, institutions, communities and the political arena. Whitmore (2011) shares his belief that coaching has the ability to support individuals in accessing their inner wisdom to use the knowledge we have as a species more wisely.

Furthermore, coaching is transient by nature and it might be that this factor contributes to the quality of the relationship. In support of the limited timeframe of coaching, Cox (2010) raises a noteworthy factor in the coaching relationship, which is often overlooked, namely preparing for the ending of the relationship. As Cox (2010) suggests, once the objectives have been achieved the coaching relationship comes to a conclusion. Cox (2010) goes on to proffer sound advice to coaches, suggesting that a good ending is one that is planned for at the outset and incorporated into the coaching contract, thus avoiding any potential difficulties on the way, such as creating a dependency on the coach. Kahn (2011) concurs with this sentiment, although he suggests we never reach a point where there is no more insight or learning to be gained as opportunities for growth occur throughout life. However, from a perspective of integrity, it is important that the coach remains within the boundaries of the initial contract and if the objectives or outcomes are achieved, the relationship should either be terminated or a new contract established. However, should the latter be the chosen path, the coach needs to be conscious of the danger of dependency, which could include a dependency of the coachee on the coach or the need on the part of the coach to sustain the relationship. Compatibility often surfaces when an organization or individual makes the decision to engage in coaching. There are arguments for and against a coach having knowledge of the particular sector of a client organization. One of the advantages are that the coach is already equipped with knowledge and understanding of the issues and challenges faced by the organization. One of the disadvantages is that accompanying such knowledge might also be assumptions that go unchallenged. McComb (2012) raises an interesting consideration and suggests that the coach and coachee should not be overly compatible as it is likely to lead to complacency and lack of challenge of the coachee.

However, there is a potential dark side to the coaching relationship and its potential for exercising power. As Welman and Bachkirova (2010) point out, there is inherent within everyone the potential desire to impose their will on someone else. Power can be seductive and Michel Foucault (2006) argues throughout his writings that the misuse of power is the source of most of the evils to be found within society. De Haan (2011) raises a very interesting aspect of the potential darker side of the relationship and urges the coach to be aware of the influence of transference and counter-transference in the coaching relationship which could also provide insight into parallel processes going on in the organization or elsewhere in the context of the coachee. He goes so far as to say that coaches ignore the possible awareness of this phenomenon at their own peril. As coach, our response to and perspectives of a coachee could very well be the same as others would experience when interacting with them, which could be a rich source of creating self-awareness for the coachee.

Power as a concept permeating organizational theories and practices is well documented. The power dynamic between the coach and the coachee is particularly significant in the successful outcome of the coaching relationship. Furthermore, the debate on power within the coaching relationship extends beyond that encountered between the coach and coachee and needs to include the dynamics within the organization (du Toit and Sim, 2010). In our paper (Reissner and du Toit, 2011) we both challenge and explore the possible use and abuse of power within the complex relationship of coaching, which makes multiple opportunities for the use and abuse of power possible. An example is that the coach may see themselves in the role of expert or this exalted status may be conferred upon them by their clients. The relationship is therefore open to the possible use and abuse of power, which according to Linstead (2004) is an enduring aspect of human relationships. Furthermore, coaching is increasingly used as a management development tool which may therefore be used in the pursuit of self-interest and the exploitation of others, even though it is not necessarily a clear and conscious decision to do so. We identify three main power dynamics which may be involved in the coaching process: (1) the personal power of the coach to convince the organization about their expertise and to work with the coachee as part of the coaching assignment; (2) the power of the organization to sell the story of the need for coaching to both the coach and the coachee; (3) the coachee's power to sell their own story to both the coach and the organization. Storytelling is an integral part of the evolution of mankind and is natural, innocent but often unacknowledged (McAdams, 1997). However, it has the ability to exert power over others, manipulate, distort and abuse (Gabriel, 2004; Lapp and Carr, 2008) and make a powerful contribution to the complex social and power dynamics in organizations. We suggest that there are four possible stages in the coaching process where there is the possibility for the abuse of power (Reissner and du Toit, 2011: 248):

> *contracting stage*, in which the coach will sell their services to the organization, convincing them of their approach, reputation and credentials while the organization will sell their need for coaching to the coach in search of the right appointment;

> *selection stage*, in which the organization will sell the idea of coaching to the employee in question (coachee), convincing them of the need for or potential benefits of coaching. The coach may be asked to support this process by telling and selling their own story to the potential coachee;

> *coaching stage*, in which coach and coachee interact and in which the coachee rewrites their story and sells it to themselves;

dissemination stage, in which this new story will be sold to other stakeholders in the organization to convince them of the need for change and to make it happen.

As I discussed in Chapter 3, from a critical perspective one could question whether the absence of judgement and the emphasis on support may prevent the coach from challenging the assumptions and beliefs of the coachee. This may lead to collusion with the coachee in maintaining their status quo. Instead, I discuss the value of postmodernism to coaching which is based on a philosophy of scepticism and challenge. A further potential for abusing the relationship is for the coach to impose the models and techniques they favour for the coaching intervention on a coachee possibly vulnerable to the perceived superior suggestions of the coach. In the oftentimes complex and ambiguous environments faced by the coachee, the temptation for the coach is to revert to that which is familiar and comfortable, ignoring the particular set of circumstances of the coachee (Cavanagh and Lane, 2012). Instead, the approach should be that of the systemic eclectic coach (Clutterbuck and Megginson, 2011), which supports the coachee with the particular approach relevant to their circumstances and not what is the stock models and techniques of the coach. The discussions in Chapter 7 on constructionism provide the awareness and understanding which facilitates a mindset comfortable with ambiguity and uncertainty. This is made possible through cross-discipline collaboration, which I argue is another reason for the emerging profession to guard against creating an elitism of what constitutes coaching and therefore what is included and excluded in the practice or the metanarrative I referred to in the previous chapter on the discussion of philosophy. This is supported by Cavanagh and Lane (2012: 83), who suggest that it is through collaboration that innovation and creativity emerge. 'Hence, part of the challenge facing us as practitioners is to remain open to, and genuinely engage with, other perspectives – particularly those that seem furthest from our own.'

An added dimension to the coaching relationship is that of the internal coach. Organizations have recognized the value of coaching and are finding different ways of disseminating the benefits throughout their organizations. Coaching has traditionally focused on external coaches brought in to support the top teams, but organizations are now endeavouring to instil a coaching culture within their organizations by creating an internal coaching capacity. Swathes of employees are selected to undergo various forms of training and development to act as internal coaches. It is true that internal coaches are more readily available and accessible and understand internal politics and organizational knowledge. They also offer a more cost-effective solution to the organization than paying the fees of an external coach. They are also in a better position to observe the coachee in their organizational environment, thereby providing feedback to the coachee based on direct observation in their natural habitat. However, there are also a number of concerns, as follows. The first is related to the relationship and credibility of the internal coach. There are issues of contracting in terms of who is the client; the organization or the coachee. The second issue is to do with confidentiality and ownership of the issues raised during the coaching relationship. The initial contracting will have to be specific in terms of how the information that will emerge during the coaching relationship is to be treated. Finally, there are issues around loyalty from the perspective of the internal coach. The organization pays the salary of the internal coach and it raises questions whether the coach will find their loyalties divided at some stage of the coaching provision.

I discussed the role of philosophy to coaching at length in the previous chapter, which leads me to have reservations whether an internal coach has the ability to provide the challenge necessary to allow the organization to question its practices, values and behaviours. Brockbank and McGill (2006) support this challenge and state that such a scheme is less likely to stimulate transformation, innovation and creativity. Based on the model by Burrell and Morgan (1979) identifying a reality dimension along a subjectivism/objectivism continuum, Brockbank and McGill (2006) argue that transformation of an individual or organization will be achieved only if existing views and the status quo is challenged. However, there is no doubt that organizations benefit from creating a coaching culture, but for it to achieve the level of challenge and reflection associated with coaching, some of these issues need to be raised and discussed as part of establishing a coaching culture.

TRUST

Trust as a key element in the quality of the coaching relationship is supported in the coaching literature by numerous
authors (Jones and Spooner, 2006; Luebbe, 2005; Whybrow,
2008). The theme of trust is associated with a person-centred
approach and there is a general acceptance that modern-day
coaching psychology has its roots in the person-centred
approach of Carl Rogers (1967), who argues that trust is a vital
component in such a relationship. De Haan (2008) emphasizes
that the success of coaching is reliant on a strong trusting relationship between the coach and coachee and not the techniques
and models applied by the coach. Trust, according to Rogers
(1967), allows for an openness and transparency through which
a person is able to express their feelings and vulnerabilities and
which may ultimately lead to self-actualization. An environment of trust allows the client to express themselves, their ideas
and emotions without the fear of judgement or retribution. The
opportunity of having the time to talk about things that affect
them individually, working through these with someone they
have built a trusting relationship with, seems to be one of the
biggest benefits of coaching. Rogers (1967) suggests that when
the teacher has the capacity to understand the student from
within and with a sensitive awareness of the way in which the
learner experiences the process of learning, the likelihood of
significant learning is increased. In his book, De Haan (2008)
draws on the work of Carlberg, who identifies moments such
as these as 'turning point moments'. De Haan's research
attempts to identify the effectiveness of coaching and the contribution of these 'critical incidents'. Whatever we may wish to
call these moments, it is clear that the quality of the relationship between the coach and the coachee has to operate at a
deep level of trust in order to make these moments possible.

THE PRESENCE OF THE COACH

In an attempt to identify the special nature of the relationship,
O'Neill (2000) argues that presence is one of the most important
principles and tools of coaching. This is supported by others

(Brockbank and McGill, 2006; Kauffman, 2008; Whybrow, 2008) who suggest that how the coach 'shows up' in the coaching relationship will determine the perceived value of coaching. Silsbee (2008) concurs and goes on to suggest that the importance of presence within coaching is arguably a key requirement in the effectiveness of the coach to cultivate real and lasting change for the client. Silsbee (2008: 21) perceives 'presence' as 'a state of awareness, in the moment, characterized by the felt experience of timelessness, connectedness, and a larger truth'. He argues that being present allows the individual to maximize their resourcefulness and optimizes their responsiveness to the circumstances they find themselves in. A further aspect of the presence of the coach is suggested by Augustijnen et al. (2011) who introduce the notion of the right attitude on the part of the coach as necessary for a good relationship and providing a secure environment for the coachee to engage in self-reflection and change. Another attitude they suggest is that of self-disclosure on the part of the coach as is found in the therapeutic relationship and thereby establishing the coach as a role model to stimulate the self-efficacy of the coachee to aid them in finding solutions to particular issues or problems.

The notion of being in the moment is also reflected in the work of Csikszentmihalyi (2002), a proponent of positive psychology and who argues that the attention we bring to a situation and related activity will determine the quality of our experience thereof. He argues that the deep level of concentration or attention we bring to a situation or experience creates a state of flow, leading to a sense of harmony. I suggest therefore that the intention, attitude and expectations of the coach are paramount in creating the quality of the relationship. This leads me on to an increased discussion of mindfulness in the coaching literature. De Haan (2012: 200) associates mindfulness as a spiritual faculty in Buddhism which refers to an attentive awareness of the reality of things, which includes not only a spiritual experience but also 'awareness of one's sensations, feelings, thoughts, perceptions, and consciousness itself'.

At the time of writing, the coaching conversations at conferences, articles and general discussions as to what is 'new' in coaching is awash with ideas of mindfulness. In essence, mindfulness is about our ability and willingness to be fully engaged in whatever situation we may find ourselves in, and has strong resonance with the ideas of Csikszentmihalyi (2002) and the ability of being in the state of flow. Done well, mindfulness is not merely a technique or practice, but a way of being. The sentiments of mindfulness resonate with coaching, such as the ability to observe without criticism, which makes it a practice worthy of exploration by the coach who is conscious about the way they show up in their coaching sessions.

THE READINESS TO BE COACHED

A further critical factor in the success of the coaching relationship is the readiness of the coachee to be coached (Bachkirova, 2007), which resonates with the literature of transformational learning proposed by Mezirow (1981). A further aspiration of coaching is that the coaching relationship is one where the coach is absorbed by the coachee without judgement and what it is that makes the coachee tick, what their passions are, and providing the tools for learning to enable them to achieve the results they want. This is the suggested attitude of the therapist referred to by Kelly (1991) in relation to his postulates of personal construct psychology and referred to in Chapter 4. In order to realize this, Grant (2007) perceives coaching as being a robust and challenging intervention strategy for the purpose of delivering tangible benefits. However, as a constructionist, I would caution against the motivation and ownership of certain benefits. The perceived value the coachee assigns to coaching may very well be intangible and contradict the benefits of other interested parties, such as the organization, and may pose an ethical dilemma for the coach. This is an example of the importance of contracting at the outset of the coaching relationship and the determination of who the client is and how priority is to be assigned to perceived outcomes.

Rogers (1967) also proposes that the educator, or coach, would be much more effective if they were to demonstrate realness or genuineness when entering into a relationship with the learner without front or façade. They should therefore express and communicate the feelings and awareness they experience, should it be appropriate. It means they may enter into a direct personal encounter with the learner, person-to-person. As Rogers (1967) describes, it would mean that the coach is *being* themself, not denying any aspect of their identity or experience. The challenge and support of coaching is reliant on a sincere curiosity on the part of the coach which, according to Whitworth et al. (1998), can lead to some unexpected and significant discoveries. Through curious questioning of the situation of the coachee the coach facilitates the process of self-discovery and learning within the coachee. The power of questioning is discussed in a later chapter in relation to transformational learning, and as Mezirow (1990) suggests, it is through critical questioning and reflective practice that transformation of deep-seated assumptions occur. Transformation has to be preceded by awareness, which then opens up the opportunity for different choices leading to changes and transformation of thinking and behaviours.

An overarching assumption of coaching, however, is that the agenda of the intervention is driven by the coachee who therefore has the ultimate say in the outcome of the process (Wilson, 2007). If sustainable change and transformation is to occur, ownership of the outcome has to reside with the coachee. Furthermore, such ownership also prevents any possible dependency the coachee may develop in relation to the coach. An equal partnership of the coaching relationship is also a significant factor of adult learning, as discussed in a subsequent chapter. Wilson (2007) goes on to suggest that the role of a coach is that of a person who enables the individual to gain self-knowledge with the assumption that this would lead to a more fulfilled personal and professional life. The role of the coach in supporting awareness of self on behalf of the coachee is congruent with the relationship between the learner and educator as proposed by Mezirow (1990). Stein (2009) suggests that self-awareness leads to self-observation which enables the individual to make different choices in relation to their thoughts and behaviours. A significant expectation of coaching is that self-awareness within the coached individual is achieved through skilful questioning that helps to surface deep-seated assumptions within the coachee.

COACHING SPACE

My experience and research suggests that the coaching 'space' is more than merely a physical one and that it is also perceived as a psychological place the coachee could return to between coaching sessions. The process of coaching therefore continues beyond the actual time spent with the coach. The authentic space is a key feature in psychology, and the person-centred coaching psychologist, for example, argues that by accepting the coachee in a non-judgemental and authentic space, they will be self-determining and motivated to achieve their optimal level of functioning (Joseph and Bryant-Jefferies, 2007; Wilson, 2007). Furthermore, many coaches as well as coachees suggest that in this space time appears to be suspended. Csikszentmiha-lyi (2002) suggests that being in the flow he refers to is when time stands still for that person and the outside world does not exist as all of their attention and energy is focused on the particular activity they are engaged in. He goes on to suggest that the process of total involvement with a particular experience creates this state of flow, which he suggests leads to the achievement of control of our inner lives.

When as coaches we enter the coaching room or the psychological space which is the coaching space, a different set of rules apply. For example, it is important for the coach to strive to set aside their own prejudices and to approach the coachee without judgement, as we have seen from other discussions. As argued by Kelly (1991) in relation to the psychotherapy relationship and which equally applies to the coach, in order to achieve the space referred to, the therapist needs to subsume their reality in favour of that of the client for the purpose of understanding the client and the client's motivations. Some of those rules may be assumed rather than being made explicit, but it is part of a psychological contract. However, before a coach can create that space they need to have a good relationship with the coachee which reflects mutual respect. In order to keep this space 'sacred', it is important that the participants honour and respect those rules. One coachee commented on how she perceived the coaching space:

VIGNETTE

It is all about you and you have to get into that space that it is all about you, but not in a selfish way, but in a self responsibility way.

Another way of identifying the special nature of this space discussed above is to refer to the work of Stern (2004), who focuses on the importance of the therapist in psychotherapy to be with the client in the moment. He describes the 'now' as moments of intensity that may last for only seconds, but these powerful seconds may reveal deep understanding of self to the individual. Through working with the coachee in the here and now, the coachee is able to become aware of deep-seated subjective knowledge, which may fundamentally impact on how they live their life. The value of such a state is also referred to by Rogers (1980), who suggests that the relationship between therapist and client transcends itself to become something larger and which includes a profound energy of growth and healing.

The space referred to facilitates the capacity to listen deeply, which is widely accepted as one of the key ingredients to successful coaching as argued by de Vries et al. (2007). Whitworth et al. (1998) identify such listening as not only listening to the words spoken by the coachee, but also what is behind the words and even the spaces in between the words. They also argue that in order to achieve deep listening, it is necessary to draw on one's intuition. They perceive intuition as an intelligence, which can arguably be developed. Rogers (1980) talks movingly of his experiences with clients both in therapy and also with executives on the power of being heard. He suggests that when he hears not only the words spoken by a client, but their own private and personal meaning, many things happen. Rogers (1980) suggests that it is as though the person once again becomes a human being, as someone has truly *heard* what it is like to be that person. Therefore how the coach and coachee interact within the coaching space is a significant component of what they identify as the process of coaching. Cavanagh and Lane (2012) add that given the possible position of power of the coach within the coaching relationship, it is the responsibility of the coach to create a strong holding space which allows the coachee to explore the anxieties, ambiguities and complexities they may bring to coaching.

I have not discussed the actual physical space of coaching as there are no set criteria available as to what makes for a good coaching space. Where discussed, the focus of the coaching space tends to centre on the psychological space of coaching and the necessity of creating such a space in order for the coachee to feel safe and heard. However, it is necessary for a coach to think about the contribution of the physical space as a learning environment for the coachee to reflect on whatever the agenda is that they bring to coaching. Although obvious, it is necessary to take into account the noise level if a public area is to act as the coaching space. I have a personal preference not to coach clients in their offices or place of work as having a physical distance between them and their organizations can assist in creating a different perspective of their working environment. In addition there are the practical implications of the place of work, such as interruptions from colleagues, phone calls and the arrival of incoming emails, all of which act as distractors from the coaching conversation. Different coaches and coachees will have different preferences when choosing the physical space and I would suggest that it is one of the items for discussion when contracting with the client, and should be regularly reviewed and a new venue found if required.

CONCLUSION

This chapter has introduced some of the key issues a coach needs to consider before they embark on any coaching contract with a client. Giving attention and thought to some of these issues will go a long way to avoiding misunderstanding emerging later on in the coaching process. What I have not discussed are the techniques and models of the coach and, as I have made clear in the introductory chapter, this text is not about developing or favouring specific models or techniques. There is a plethora of books and articles on the market which will allow the coach to develop their own particular brand and approach to coaching. The chapters to follow will explore what I have identified as the 'black box' of coaching.

THE TOOLS OF SENSEMAKING

5

CHAPTER OBJECTIVES

- Understand the different aspects of sensemaking
- The role of sensemaking in coaching
- Explore the connection between sensemaking and groupthink
- Challenging the sensemaking process through critical coaching

INTRODUCTION

To support the parallel I draw between coaching and sensemaking, I find inspiration from the work of Karl Weick, the theorist who is particularly associated with the notion of sensemaking. He has made an extensive study of how people make sense of events, particularly within an organizational setting. In order for an organization to function as an entity, there is a need for consensus amongst individuals who constitute the particular organization; organizational sensemaking helps to achieve such shared meaning. In explaining the process of sensemaking, Weick (1979) draws on the activity of cartography. The map will reflect the specific aspects the cartographer wants to portray; however, the map is not an exact copy of a particular terrain as there are an infinite number of plausible maps that can be constructed. The same is true of sensemaking. The picture sketched by a sensemaker does not correspond to a pre-existing reality and will therefore reflect only that which the sensemaker chooses to focus on.

Although he is a psychologist, Weick (1979) has applied much of his research and writing for the purpose of understanding the sensemaking process in organizations. He suggests that despite the illusion of logic, objectivity and concreteness, organizations, like people, are saturated with subjectivity, guesses and make-do. Above all, Weick (1979) perceives many of the ills that plague organizations to be of their own doing. He argues that the purpose of organizational activities is to aid its members to create order from the ambiguity and the complexity in which they find themselves. Furthermore, Weick goes on to suggest that organizations often reconstruct history after the event to explain the position of the organization despite the fact that such histories were not the cause of the current position it may face. Weick refers to sensemaking as a retrospective activity, which I will discuss in more detail below.

We could apply the same principles to coaching and argue that people seek the support of coaching to help them to make sense of the ambiguity they are confronted with. The sensemaking the coach and coachee engage in is also a process of retrospective sensemaking. The face-to-face interaction offered by the coaching intervention aids the coachee in reducing the complexity they face and allows for the product of sensemaking to be integrated with their existing frames of references. Alternatively, where necessary, coaching supports the individual in restructuring the frames of references to accommodate and integrate new and more enabling ways of looking at the world and dealing with such complexities and ambiguities. Coaching also confronts the structures and realities that have been invented during past sensemaking activities and which may no longer be relevant or even appropriate for different circumstances the coachee may be experiencing. As we have discussed in previous chapters, the special nature of the coaching space created during coaching provides both the support and challenge to enable the coachee to engage in the self-reflection. The supportive environment and the relationship of trust created between the coach and coachee facilitates increasing awareness and availability of options.

Weick suggests we are over-reliant on the habitual and routine responses to familiar situations and these responses are then interrupted when we are faced with complexity or situations that challenge previous sensemaking. Psychology refers to this state as cognitive dissonance and if we are to cope with change it is necessary for us to integrate the novel with the familiar. Alternatively, we may have to revisit our views of the situation and change or adapt the schema we apply in order to make sense of the world. A motivating driver for a person to seek the support of coaching may be due to the fact that they are experiencing tension between their internal schema and the challenges exacted on it by a particular change to their otherwise familiar circumstances. There is often reference made to the perceived view that people resist change, particularly in relation to organizational change. However, this perception could also be understood as people engaged in the process of coming to terms with the tensions of integrating new perspectives into their existing schemas. There are many reasons why the support of coaching is sought and seeking help in dealing with that which is unfamiliar is one such motivation.

As we have seen with the economic downturn experienced at the time of writing and which began with the demise of Northern Rock in 2008, a willingness to entertain the unbelievable sometimes goes unheeded at our peril and is often because of collective groupthink that rejects what is perceived as incomprehensible and unimaginable (du Toit and Sim, 2010). The study of groupthink was brought to the fore by the work of Janis (1972). He identified a number of antecedents he perceived as preceding groupthink. These included high levels of cohesiveness in the group, defects in the structure leading to the insulation of the particular group, the absence of leader impartiality, lack of procedural norms, strong member homogeneity, and provocative situational factors such as high stress levels. Janis suggested that the cohesiveness of the group was the most important factor in creating the notion of groupthink. The familiar symptoms of groupthink outlined by Janis include the collective rationalization in the group, pressure on individual group members to conform, emergence of mind guards who take it upon themselves to ensure contradictory information is marginalized, a sense of infallibility, the illusion of unanimity and self censorship. In order to sustain the beliefs of the group it requires the collusion of not only those within the group but sometimes external parties as well.

By way of demonstration, the banking sector is a fascinating case study in both the destructive power of groupthink as well as the collusion that has reinforced the destructive behaviour of the sector as a whole.

As discussed in Chapter 3 on philosophy, the coaching practice, which draws inspiration from the philosophy of scepticism, may have the potential of acting as an antidote to groupthink in organizations. Coaching has the ability to challenge practices of groupthink and the destructive sensemaking processes within a group which demonstrates the symptoms of groupthink as outlined above. Janis went on to suggest that counteracting groupthink included extensive use of critical evaluators in policy-forming groups. Translated into organizational parlance this would mean drawing on the support of a critical coach to challenge the collective sensemaking of a group demonstrating some of the elements of groupthink. It is clear from the evidence that it is near impossible for group members to query their own group norms. Instead it requires an external source such as the critical coach to provide the impetus for this to occur.

The greater the variety of believable possibilities we have in our repertoire the more solutions we will be able to draw on when dealing with the unknown. This reflects the law of requisite variety as put forward by Ashby (Conant and Ashby, 1970) which suggests that if we are to grasp and deal with the variation presented by the ongoing flow of events, our thoughts and actions must be equally varied. Weick (1995) goes on to suggest that the richer one's language the richer the resultant reflective thought and ultimately the choices at one's disposal. Weick (1995) offers a cautionary note to the labels we assign to events as these may assume the status of a truth and therefore not reflect an openness to change. However, Weick argues that the whole point of sensemaking is to challenge such labels of belief. However, as he states: 'Once something is labelled a problem, that is when the problem starts' (1995: 90). The power of beliefs is that they may lead to self-fulfilling prophecies as they influence what we choose to pay attention to. One of the benefits of coaching is that the coach challenges the labels of the coachee and their underlying values and beliefs. Coaching therefore goes a long way in helping the coachee to think more clearly about the subconscious steps when they are engaged in sensemaking and to challenge perceived labels of truth.

During the sensemaking process, the individual filters categorize and integrate new stimuli into their existing frames of reference. The coaching space has the ability to provide the support needed in dealing with the constant bombardment of stimuli in a more conscious manner and thereby assisting the coachee in making sense of it. It also enables the individual to exercise greater choice in selecting the sense to be made (du Toit, 2007). For example, an individual may perceive only one solution or choice when faced with a particular situation. However, supported through the sensemaking process they engage in with the coach, the coachee may recognize different and alternative choices available to them. This was the experience of the following coachee:

VIGNETTE

Most barriers are self-made. I acknowledge that there are external barriers, but they are only impenetrable because you look at them from only one particular way. You need help to see that there is another equally valuable way of looking at it, which may initially cut across what you think is right or wrong or more valuable and when you keep probing, supported by coaching, you recognize that there may be another way forward.

I suggest the interaction and dialogue that takes place within the coaching relationship, and which is labelled as coaching, is the process that assists the coachee to make sense of their world. The co-constructive relationship between the coach and coachee allows them to integrate new experiences into their existing frames of reference. It reflects the retrospective nature of sensemaking which Weick (1979) refers to and which has its starting point in the assumptions formed by the individual. It also includes their conscious and unconscious expectations about a future event which generates predictions as to how the event is likely to unfold. The discrepancy between predictions and the event itself needs to be explained through sensemaking for the purpose of assigning meaning to perceived uncertainty, ambiguity and paradoxes. Problems do not necessarily present themselves with readymade solutions. Instead they have to be constructed from the matter which accompanies the problem and failure to do so may be a motivation for individuals to seek the support of coaching. When talking about sensemaking, Weick suggests (1995: 15) it is 'to talk about reality as an ongoing accomplishment that takes form when people make retrospective sense of the situations in which they find themselves and their creations'. Furthermore, he suggests that there is a strong reflective quality involved in the act of sensemaking – a cornerstone of coaching. Being a retrospective activity, the individual discovers the world on which they have already imposed their own beliefs, thereby discovering what they have previously invented.

SEVEN STAGES OF SENSEMAKING

Weick (1995) identifies seven stages of sensemaking, which I suggest is equally applicable to coaching as introduced below. Of importance to coaching is that one includes both action and context, which are seen as key aspects of sensemaking. As Weick suggests, the seven stages can also be perceived as a sequence of events. However, he cautions that it is relatively crude as it omits possible feedback loops and in certain circumstances some of the steps may not necessarily feature. However, it provides a lens through which we are able to get closer to that which transpires within the coaching relationship which makes it so powerful and transforming for the coachee.

1. Grounded in Identity Construction

Weick (1995: 18) suggests that sensemaking 'begins with a sensemaker'. However, he argues that an individual sensemaker never makes sense in isolation. I introduce the concepts of constructionism in a later chapter, and as will become apparent, constructionism argues that our identities emerge through the process of interaction. Gergen (1991) also refers to multiple identities, or the pastiche personality, which results from numerous interactions in different circumstances; these are identities that are in a continual state of construction and reconstruction. Gergen (1991) argues that we do an injustice to the complexity and variety of human nature if we perceive an individual to have only one identity. Oftentimes the coachee will be subject to internal conflict as a result of multiple identities vying for centre stage and the opportunity to express the needs of that particular identity. The many identities may include that of employee, family member and numerous others unique to a particular individual, which, as I said, may at times be in conflict with each other. Coaching provides the space through which the coachee is able to harmonize the needs and expectations of their different identities. In the following remarks a coachee suggests how through the interaction with the coach they discovered parts of their identity which may have been hidden from view up to that point:

VIGNETTE

Hearing yourself say things, I think, did I really say that, where did that come from? So profound really.

Whatever the individual perceives their identity to be, it will effect what they perceive as being external to them. Of further value to coaching is that, as Weick (1995) suggests, people gain self-knowledge by projecting themselves into their environment and learning from the feedback this generates. A coach may suggest that the coachee experiments with different behaviours that support them in making sense of their identities or in the construction of new aspects of their identity. Furthermore, as the individual defines what they perceive as being outside of themselves, it will also change depending on the particular aspect of their identity which dominates at the time. Bruner (1991) concurs and suggests that people both react to and are shaped by their environment whilst influencing and contributing to the environment they experience. Constructionism therefore argues that we are the creators of our circumstances through our actions past and present, a notion we sometimes vehemently reject as it means we have to take ownership and responsibility for our experiences. Through the interaction with the coach the coachee brings to consciousness the assumptions and expectations they may hold of a particular situation and unravels what their contribution has been to it. Should they change or adapt those assumptions, their perspective of a particular situation will change thereby freeing them up to engage with it differently. One way in which the coach facilitates this process of sensemaking is through challenging questioning techniques. As a coachee reveals, this process is not always a pleasant or comfortable experience:

VIGNETTE

In my experience, the shift in my thinking would not have happened without the questioning techniques used by the coach and the challenging nature of the questioning. You may not necessarily like every question that they put to you, but when you go away and reflect on it and come back it seems to take your thoughts forward or at least allows you to think about why it is you act or behave in a certain way. However, that challenge isn't always comfortable. It can be painful, but it is possible because of the support of the coach. You also know that the coach has no agenda other than to support you.

As Weick (1995) suggests, our identities are sustained socially from our participation and membership of our societies or institutions such as organizations. The consistency of our identity is reflected in the identity of the organization. If the organization changes so does the identity of the individual and it may require either a redefinition of the organizational identity or that of the individual if the changing image of the organization challenges or is in conflict with their personal identity. The identity of the coachee is therefore work in progress and in a continual journey of redefinition and discovery of self which is reflected in the coaching intervention.

2. Retrospective

Weick (1995) argues that it is only after the event that we have an understanding of what it is we did or what we have experienced. He goes on to suggest that the perceived world is in fact a world in the past. As soon as we become aware of an experience it is already in the past; it is the retrospective action of capturing a moment in the continuous flow of the present. Furthermore, Weick et al. (2005) add that since sensemaking is a retrospective activity, complete accuracy in the recall and interpretation of events is therefore not possible. Due to the ever-changing and shifting nature of reality Weick (1995) argues that our perceptions of reality can never be accurate. A further contributing factor is that every individual will select different aspects of a particular reality based on their own unique filters that we each draw on in the sensemaking process. What we therefore need to focus on instead is our interpretations of reality as these will in turn influence the nature of our experiences and therefore our reactions to the perceived world in which we find ourselves. Weick (1995) argues that in the postmodern world with conflicting and ever-changing identities and realities, accuracy seems pointless and not worthy of pursuit.

Our identities help to determine the meaning we make of particular experiences and events and as identity is unique and individual our particular interpretation of an event may differ from the interpretation of another. What follows then is the activity of negotiation in an attempt to influence others to our particular way of thinking. Ongoing negotiation between parties for the purpose of establishing shared meaning is a constant within the organizational environment. For individuals or groups within an organizational context to achieve a common understanding they often have to renegotiate their interpretations of situations. The difficulty occurs when as a result of the renegotiation they have to challenge personal or individual sensemaking and therefore their associated identities as discussed above. As we mature and evolve as individuals so will our personal identity change and along with it the interpretation and the meaning we ascribe to a particular situation. The reflection facilitated by coaching will influence the meaning an individual makes retrospectively of different situations.

Meaning is therefore fluid and not a fixture of a particular event or situation. This can be both frightening and empowering depending on our particular point of view. It can be frightening if we seek certainty and meaning outside of ourselves and in some circumstances we can assign the blame for our experiences to a particular object or person. Alternatively, uncertainty can be perceived as empowering when we recognize that meaning and truth is what we create for ourselves and that at any given time it can be renegotiated. This is evident in the experience of one coachee, as follows:

VIGNETTE

The most effective part of coaching for me is the reflection, thinking about things and also having some help with that reflection. The coach helps you to focus on what is relevant and what isn't relevant. When I hear the ideas and conclusions I draw about the situation I reflect on with the coach I often comment that of course I knew that but I can only come to know that through the reflection facilitated by my coach.

Weick (1995) makes an interesting observation when he suggests that gaining clarity about an event is not dependent on gathering yet more information, but instead what is required is clarity about the preferences and values an individual draws on to make sense of an event or experience. This is precisely what coaching is able to facilitate; supporting the individual to understand how their values and assumptions influence their interpretation of events. As Weick argues, the sense we make retrospectively will in turn influence and determine our behaviours when we return to that situation and engage with it once again. Furthermore, we will also gain awareness and understanding of how and why we interact with other similar events in the way that we do. Armed with this awareness we are then able to change and adapt our actions or behaviours due to the retrospective meaning creation in which we have engaged. Furthermore, the retrospective meaning made of past activities will in turn influence the meanings we will assign to future events.

3. Enactive of Sensible Environments

It is understandable that the process we engage in to gain clarity of what we have sensed requires the involvement of our senses (Weick, 1995). As suggested by sensemaking, the environment we find ourselves in comes into being through our enactment with it. It is a reciprocal and co-creative relationship between us as individuals and the environment and circumstances we engage with. We construct that which we expect to experience, thereby creating self-fulfilling prophecies. Weick (1995) suggests that our enacted world is not only tangible, but also subjective as it has its origins in our mental models and connected to the categories we draw on to create the artefacts in the first place. These ideas form the core principles of cognitive behavioural coaching. As suggested above, the world is not a pre-given, but constantly becoming through our actions and interactions with it (Varela et al., 1991).

Huzzard (2004) concurs with Weick and suggests that sensemaking is also reliant on dealing with equivocality rather than certainty. The ability to make sense of new situations may very well require the sensemaker to disrupt taken-for-granted sense made previously, or as Pratt (2000) describes it, sensebreaking. The environment we create in turn places constraints on any future actions we may take. We engage with our environment, we create rules that in turn will determine what we expect our behaviours to be in order to comply with those rules. An excellent example of this is, at the time of writing, the economic depression experienced across the world. The perception of the recession as a reality external to people creates rules that govern behaviour such as the reluctance to spend and the need to be frugal, which in turn contributes to maintaining an economic reality labelled as a recession. Should spending and lending increase the perception of the economic situation and a possible new reality might be created, suggesting that the recession is waning. We are therefore not victims of a monolithic and fixed environment that is detached from us but we are very much part of that environment and how it comes to be, including the opportunities and constraints we associate with it.

Within the coaching relationship the coach challenges the individual to recognize and accept their particular contributions which may empower them to step out of a victim mentality and their collusion in maintaining a particular status quo. As Weick points out the world as it is experienced is both tangible as well as subjective because it is through our interaction and response to the environmental artefacts, interpretations and expectations that we contribute in creating a new environment or maintaining the status quo of an existing reality. It is worth pointing out that the interaction with the environment is not limited to the actions we take; action taken at the wrong time or the wrong action, assumptions, fears, values and beliefs with which we approach a given situation all equally contribute to the outcome.

4. Social

The shared meaning we create within the various communities and societies we inhabit, such as organizations, is sustained in numerous ways. One is through a common language, as is the social interaction we engage in for the purpose of maintaining our communities and societies. Proponents of sensemaking suggest that socialization is the milieu within which our sensemaking takes place. We may be influenced by the sense made of others and in turn shape and influence their own sensemaking activities. However, the social process is not limited to talking and conversations, but includes the values, frames of reference and meanings we assign to situations.

Weick (1995) states that the context within which people make sense of their world is an important factor as it has a strong influence on what will eventually be experienced as reality. Bruner (1990) is in accord and suggests that an understanding of the social context provides the norms and standards by which new experiences are measured. It also creates the rules and expectations of the behaviours of those within the particular group or community. Furthermore, he proposes that a central theme of human psychology is the conflict we encounter in meaning-making and the necessary transactions we engage in to construct such meaning. He goes on to suggest that human life and mind are not shaped by biological factors alone, but by human constructed cultural environments as well.

Another way of interpreting the socially negotiated creation of meaning is as an act of storytelling, as suggested by Boje et al. (1999). This supports the ideas of Colville et al. (1999), that rhetoric is involved in the process of sensemaking and the sense made is therefore a matter of words that represent reality. Narrative therefore acts as the vehicle through which our understanding of the world comes into being. Both the recounting and listening to stories have been significant tools in the evolution through which human beings have learned and developed. It is also through narrative and dialogue within our relationships that we create our identities (Gergen, 1991). Through the collaborative process of narrative and storytelling we are able to critically assess prevailing assumptions and meanings. Consequently, it is through the sharing of stories that we gain insight into how others make sense of the world and the assumptions that underpin their beliefs. Grisham (2006) concludes that politicians, artists, philosophers and playwrights have successfully crafted stories throughout the centuries for the purpose of transferring knowledge, eliciting emotive feelings as well as employing it as a power for persuasion. Within the coaching environment the coach pays particular attention to the conversation, narrative and stories told by the coachee and how these are communicated, for example the accompanying emotions, as it helps to provide an insight into the reality of the coachee. I will introduce the role storytelling plays in coaching in a subsequent chapter.

5. Ongoing

As Weick argues throughout his writing, sensemaking is a process that is without beginning or end; it is a continuous flow of meaning creation. He goes on to suggest that we are constantly revising and building provisional assumptions which will in turn influence future sensemaking activities. As suggested above, we engage in ongoing sensemaking through conversation, storytelling, narration and linguistic abilities, which all play a part in the process of making sense of the complexity and ambiguity we operate in. If sensemaking is perceived as an ongoing, social process it could be argued that the future is unpredictable as well as being unknown. Through the ongoing conversations and narrations we engage in with others, we jointly make sense of the unknown which helps to create the reality we will come to experience at a given time.

Weick (1995) suggests that we only become aware of this flow when it is interrupted, which is often accompanied by an emotional reaction. The awareness of interruption signals that changes in the environment have occurred. Those emotions may be either positive or negative, depending on the nature of the changes or the interpretation of those changes, which in turn will influence subsequent sensemaking. As I have discussed in other chapters, emotions are a significant part of coaching as they provide clues not only to the coach but also to the coachee, as to their values, beliefs and assumptions the coachee may have about the world, their place in that world and what they may perceive as reality.

6. Focused on by Extracted Cues

Weick (1995) suggests that the process of sensemaking is rapid, and therefore in order to observe people making sense of situations such as paradoxes, dilemmas or events they cannot immediately explain, we need to observe them doing so. We can also experience this in the way that people notice situations, the cues they extract and how they may embellish on those extracted cues. Situations such as these are often observable within the coaching environment as the coachee might wrestle with paradoxes and challenges they are unable to make sense of on their own and seek the support of the coach in order to do so. We select simple cues that provide us with a sense of familiarity and a sense of the larger sensemaking that might be happening. Such cues also provide a point of reference, which is also an important source of power as it has the ability to direct our attention.

The context within which a particular cue is noticed and the value we assign to the cue is also of significance. The cues represent familiarity and knowledge or experience we have gained from previous sensemaking activities, which in turn leads to the assumptions we make about a particular situation or circumstance. Having extracted the cue or cues we may not necessarily look further for additional evidence to confirm or refute the cues we have selected. The faith we assign to particular cues will in turn determine or influence enactment, leading to the notion of self-fulfilling prophecies. Weick refers to these cues as seeds which will lead to the eventual conclusion to a particular sensemaking process. The context will also influence what the cue will eventually become and it will also influence how a particular cue is interpreted. Cues inspire confidence in people by giving a general direction of where an individual is and where it is they want to be. We could also argue that if we select different cues, our experiences of current and future events may change. Exploring the possibility of a changed reality by focusing on different cues is made possible through the support and challenge provided by the coaching intervention.

7. Driven by Plausibility Rather than Accuracy

Accuracy is, as Weick (1995) argues, a nicety, not a necessity: 'Instead, sensemaking is about plausibility, pragmatics, coherence, reasonableness, creation, invention, and instrumentality' (Weick, 1995: 57). As discussed above, people select and filter certain cues as part of the sensemaking process and which is also dependent on the particular context within which the sensemaking takes place. Furthermore, the selection may vary from person to person, which the individual will embellish and elaborate on. A crucial element of sensemaking is that the past is a reconstruction that did not occur in the way it is remembered, explaining why there are often different versions of a given event. The writing of history is a classic example. Renditions of events will vary quite significantly by different people, depending on their position to the experience or event. Instead of pursuing the myth of accuracy, Weick (1995) suggests what is needed is a good story. Why? Because a good story is capable of holding different elements together long enough to guide and generate action. This notion reflects the central tenet of postmodernism, which suggests that the equivocal postmodern world is permeated with different interpretations, conflicting interests and populated by people with multiple and ever-changing identities. I have discussed the notion of little narratives versus a grand narrative in Chapter 3 on philosophy. Hence the value of a story; it provides themes and workable maps that could be recreated depending on the order and sense of the future.

The reason for accuracy being secondary in the analysis of sensemaking is that people will distort and filter cues so as to avoid being overwhelmed with data. Furthermore, the act of collaboration and embellishment allows interpretation to eventually surface. Different cues with different meanings from someone else would make accuracy of a particular object an impossibility. As suggested above, cues are associated with events of the past and if the past did not occur in the way that it is remembered it would make accuracy impossible and therefore meaningless. In the rapidly changing environment, especially that of organizations, if accuracy were achieved, it would be so for a short period of time only. Instead, Weick suggests stories are memorable in determining our experiences. A further powerful factor that influences such experiences is the expectations we have of given situations and anticipated events. Furthermore, the power of sensemaking in influencing the experiences we have is when it resonates with the expectations of other events which are then capable of being constructed retrospectively. Moreover, it also captures emotions and thoughts and helps to explain puzzles and energize people into action. As suggested, I will return to the value of stories and storytelling to coaching in subsequent chapters.

SENSEMAKING THROUGH ACTION

In addition to the seven stages of sensemaking as put forward by Weick, a number of proponents of sensemaking suggest that it can also be set in motion through action (Boland, 1984; Smircich and Stubbart, 1985; Weick, 1995). This supports Weick's thoughts on sensemaking, suggesting that understanding does not necessarily lead to action but instead action results in understanding. We find a similar sentiment put forward by supporters of action research such as Reason and Bradbury (2008) for example, who argue for the necessity of action in order to create understanding. It is based on the premise that the reality we experience is often the result of actions taken previously. The reality experienced is therefore firmly associated with the person engaged in enactment which supports the principles of social constructionism which I will discuss in the following chapter. Enactment casts us in the role of creators of our own environment rather than that of passive spectators. More of constructionism in subsequent chapters.

Gioia (2006), in interpreting the work of Weick (1995), goes one step further and argues that the human hand is apparent in the construction of many events that are often labelled as the result of higher forces. Boland (1984) also reflects these sentiments and suggests that through continuous enactment the environment is thus created as opposed to something that is objectively knowable. The latter reflects the sentiments of postmodernism as described in Chapter 3. Applying these ideas to organizations, Smircich and Stubbart (1985:731) state that, 'the idea of enactment underscores a view that one's own actions and the actions of others make an organization and its environment'. The essence is that, 'Individually or collectively, we create what we confront' (Gioia, 2006: 1715). The notion of enactment is also intimately bound up with ecological change. It is through the process of enactment that we as sensemakers directly engage with an external environment, which in turn bends around our enactments. I will return to the ideas of making sense through enactment and discussed in relation to the theories of adult learning, and action learning in particular, during a later chapter.

Smircich and Stubbart (1985: 724) develop the view of enactment further and suggest, 'that environments are enacted through the social construction and interaction processes of organized actors'. The same could be said of the coaching environment. In partnership the coach and coachee interact to construct meaning and explanation which emerge as a result of such interaction. As we have seen from the above discussions, Weick (1995) argues that sensemaking is an active process. He goes on to caution against associating sensemaking with some of the more passive phenomena, such as perception and representation, which accepts the environment as given. Viewed from the perspective of a realist, sensemaking would be seen as a problem of discovery, whereas the constructionist considers sensemaking as a problem of invention, a position I argue is a more enabling and empowering philosophy with which to underpin the coaching intervention.

In defining the notion of *sense*, Brown (1994) includes that of feeling, thought and meaning within a particular context as perceived by the senses – namely the faculty of perception or sensation. He goes on to argue that sensemaking can be construed as the cognitive activity that determines knowledge and understanding and, as suggested earlier, is fundamental to cognitive behavioural coaching. Sensemaking can also be perceived as the process through which we reduce the complexity of our environment down to a level that makes sense to us (Weick, 1995). Building on the idea of sensemaking as a meaning-creating activity, Dougherty et al. (2000) perceive sensemaking as the process through which information, insights and ideas coalesce into something useful, or *stick* together in a meaningful way. According to Weick (1995) sensemaking therefore suggests that the sensemaker is both the author and interpreter, creator as well as discoverer. This sentiment reflects a fundamental premise of coaching, which is to support the coachee in taking responsibility for their reality and the contribution they have made towards its manifestation.

EMOTIONS AND SENSEMAKING

Until fairly recently we have shied away from associating emotions with the serious business of organizations and its various activities. That all changed through the numerous publications of David Goleman on emotional intelligence. The result is that emotional intelligence is seen as a fundamental building block of effective leadership. Weick (1995) also suggested that the creative act of knowing is accompanied by emotions. It is through the emotional mind that we find a balance between the rational, logical and deductive form of comprehension, described by Day and Leitch (2001) as deliberate. On the other hand is the emotional mind, which is perceived as intuitive, impulsive and described by some as illogical. Irrespective of our awareness of them, emotions are intricately connected with many areas of our functioning. The inclusion of emotions in human activities is supported by others and in particular as a significant element in adult learning, as I will discuss in later chapters. In fact, Neale et al. (2009) assert that the experiential triangle of thoughts, emotions and actions is present in everything we do. The coach also recognizes the value of emotions in the process of sensemaking engaged in by the coachee. This reflects the experience shared by the coach below, which suggests that the difference between coaching and other forms of learning and development is that emotions are *prerequisites* in the shift that follows coaching:

VIGNETTE

I've seen people's behaviour change and that is often not sustained because there hasn't been that attitudinal shift, that fundamental shift in beliefs, certainly how people approach things, feel about things and certain beliefs about things. So I think for transformation there has to be [an emotional] shift.

This resonates with Day and Leitch (2001), who contend that it is through our subjective and emotional world that we develop our personal constructs and meanings of our outer experiences, and the sense we make of these events and relationships. The new developments in neurophysiology of the brain provide additional insight into the fundamental role emotions play in the process of decision-making, for example when faced with a choice, and which is intimately bound up with sensemaking (Bradbury et al., 2008). These findings are also supported by authors in relation to storytelling (Allan et al., 2002; Gabriel, 2004).

In Chapter 2 I discussed the contribution of psychology and therapy to coaching, which recognizes the importance of understanding and including emotions in bringing about change. Many people enter both a therapeutic and coaching relationship with maladaptive emotions that leave them feeling stuck and often with a sense of despair. Numerous theorists, such as Greenberg and Bolger (2001), suggest that for change to happen it is first of all necessary for the individual to become aware of the emotions associated with the proposed change. Furthermore, for change to take place it is necessary for the maladaptive emotion to be replaced with a more adaptive one. Storytelling is often used within a therapeutic environment to support this process and according to Parker (2006) emotions are an important element in the telling of the story. I therefore propose that the personal act of sensemaking engaged in by the coachee will have greater meaning if the accompanying emotions are acknowledged.

THE LANGUAGE OF SENSEMAKING

A fundamental element of sensemaking is the words used in conversation, either with ourselves or with others, for the purpose of conveying the nature of our experiences. Weick suggests that before we make sense of experiences we need to see what we are thinking. This resonates with one of the key benefits of coaching, namely the space and opportunity for the coachee to reflect and therefore to 'see' what they are thinking. Words are also powerful as they reflect the meaning we associate with events and the subsequent labels we assign to these events. These labels carry with them the weight of values and beliefs which have the power to influence the associated behaviour of the coachee. Furthermore, the more entrenched the labels and their behaviours become, the more the person becomes committed to what they represent. The result is that people will find explanations to justify their behaviours and reasons for persisting with the behaviour patterns even if the outcome is negative or harmful in some way. The coaching intervention makes the sensemaking process visible by enabling the coachee to observe what is normally perceived as a subconscious process. Words are therefore significant in the cycle of thoughts, values and beliefs and behaviours. Coaching intervenes in this cycle to support the coachee by exploring and questioning the words employed by the coachee. Transforming the words used by the coachee may provide a pathway to transforming the thoughts and behaviours of the individual.

Language and its associated words are rich and dynamic and in the continuous process of changing and evolving. Language reflects the same multiplicity as the notion of our pastiche personalities put forward by Gergen (1991). The words we draw on during any of our sensemaking reflect many different vocabularies, such as those used in organizations, different professions and society at large. As suggested above, these words can reflect meaning as well as values and emotions which in turn will influence subsequent behaviours. Organizations are rife with sayings and idiosyncrasies that convey powerful and subliminal messages throughout the organization. The deep assumptions that accompany organizational language reflect the culture associated with the organization, exerting a subtle and implicit control over members of the organization. One of the core competencies of the coach is therefore their ability to listen deeply not only to the words used by the coachee but the meanings associated with those words and the impact they have on the behaviour of the individual. According to sensemaking therefore, coaching then allows the coachee to see what they are thinking and the influence of those words on their behaviour.

The use of language, particularly as it is applied in storytelling, is discussed in greater depth in the next chapter. As Weick (1995) suggests, socialization is the milieu within which our sensemaking takes place. Sensemaking includes the values, frames of references and meanings we assign to situations, which are also key aspects of the coaching process, irrespective of the tools and techniques used to challenge, question and bring them to the consciousness of the coachee. It is through the application of various tools that the coachee is supported in making sense of their world. Narrative and storytelling are powerful tools in this endeavour, which I now introduce in the next chapter.

NARRATIVE AND STORYTELLING

6

CHAPTER OBJECTIVES

- Understand the nature of storytelling
- Explore the relationship between storytelling and sensemaking
- The influence of storytelling and meaning making
- The role of storytelling in coaching

INTRODUCTION

Following on from the previous chapter on sensemaking, this chapter introduces the powerful role of narratives and story-telling as part of the sensemaking process and in particular as it relates to the coaching intervention. As we have seen in the previous chapter, instead of pursuing the myth of accuracy, Weick (1995) suggests what is needed is a good story because a good story is capable of holding different elements together long enough to guide and generate action. Stories do not offer truth, but instead verisimilitude. Stories do not provide factual information but instead they enhance and provide meaning to the facts surrounding a particular situation. The value of a story is that it provides themes and workable maps that could be rec-reated depending on the order and sense of the future. The history of storytelling is as rich and varied as the history of mankind itself and perceived as the most widely used means of communication (Bruner, 1986; McAdams, 1997; Riessman, 1993). As Kadembo (2012: 221) suggests, 'The human heritage is a story that transcends through generations: evolution, crea-tion, discoveries of places, scientific discoveries or inventions, obituaries, product profiles, organizational profiles, advertise-ments, etc.' He goes on to suggest that: 'The story reminds of the past, shapes the present and inspire for the future; hence the story is the life that was, is and will be.' Grisham concludes (2006) that politicians, artists, philosophers and playwrights have successfully crafted stories throughout the centuries for the purpose of transferring knowledge, eliciting emotive feel-ings and as a power for persuasion. In describing the nature of storytelling Gabriel (2000: 1) writes, 'Storytelling is an art of weaving, of constructing, the product of intimate knowledge.' The use of storytelling also has a rich history in being applied within an organizational context for the purpose of supporting change, communication, organizational learning and leadership development, to name but a few (Barker and Gower, 2010).

Nowhere have words greater power than in the telling of stories and it is a tradition and history which has been inti-mately connected with the evolution of mankind as I suggested above. It engages the imagination and emotions and draws the listener or reader into a co-creative relationship with the story-teller. Boje (2008) has written extensively on the nature of storytelling in organizations and identifies sensemaking as com-plex and diverse and storytelling provides a vehicle through which we can make sense of the complexities we inhabit. He goes on to suggest that an individual can at any one time make sense of many aspects and roles of themselves through interac-tion with others, whilst at the same time transcending different time frames. Boje (1995) demonstrates this through the use of the *Tamara* metaphor which he applied in describing stories that emerged from his research of the Disney Enterprise. The dozen or so characters of *Tamara*-land, presented as a stage play, enact their stories before a moving audience. The audi-ence is therefore participants in both the production as well as the consumption of the play. They are divided into small groups, moving between rooms and floors, thereby co-creating the stories that appeal to them the most. Depending on the particular characters selected by the audience, the theme or story relevant to their characters will unfold. However, a dif-ferent audience who have selected different characters will be exposed to a different set of stories and scenarios related to the same theme. As the action is simultaneous and takes place in different rooms and floors and is enacted by different characters, no audience is able to follow all of the stories. In drawing on the *Tamara* metaphor Boje (1995) demonstrates how we may select from a multiplicity of stories, dependent on the history, meaning of events, the locality, prior sequence of the stories as well as the different perspectives and interpretations of events depicted by different characters. There is therefore no single story, but many stories, depending on whose version of the story one follows. Stories are therefore in a continuous state of flux with people contributing their own interpretations, adding their own fragments to the ongoing and evolving story. Boje (1995) proposes that storytelling is a powerful mechanism through which to create a collective organizational memory and support the creation of a powerful vision of the future. Stories also have the ability to disseminate information throughout the organization and promote the culture of the organization by establishing a social context with organizational members. Many business leaders have successfully used the power of storytelling to mobilize support for their vision.

Weick (1995) also draws parallels with storytelling and goes on to suggest that it is through stories that we share the sense we make of a given situation. It also provides a mechanism that supports the communication of complex ideas. The telling of stories provides the vehicle for two or more individuals to create a collective and shared understanding of reality as perceived at a particular time. Reality as we perceive it provides a structure for our individual and collective stories. For example, through the sharing of their stories the coach and coachee engage in the sensemaking of a particular situation or challenge faced by the coachee in the collective and socially negotiated manner of storytelling as identified by Boje et al. (1999). Weick (1995) is of the opinion that stories aid comprehension as they have the ability to facilitate the integration of our known knowledge and experience with the unknown we encounter in new situations. The power of stories is that they allow us to make connections between disparate events thereby making sense of these events and providing meaning which may otherwise have eluded us. Stories are memorable and help to establish common ground with others (Barker and Gower, 2010). Furthermore, the framework provided by storytelling allows us to reconstruct the complexity associated with certain events. The telling of stories therefore has a building capacity of collectively constructing meaning by allowing the narrator and listener to share retrospection and interpretation in their collective pursuit of meaning.

EMOTIONS AND STORIES

Emotions are a powerful and significant part of storytelling as it is through the communication of emotions that we engage in the process of constructing our identity (Horrocks and Callahan, 2006). Emotions permeate daily life and are embedded in our thoughts, communications and behaviours, and fuel our motivations. We learn at a very early age and depending on the societies we grow up in, to control and censor our emotions and reveal only the emotions that are perceived as acceptable or appropriate in a given situation and set of circumstances. Through the telling and retelling of our stories we tap into the emotions that act as clues into our particular truths, identity and interpretations of events, and as we have seen from the previous chapter, this is part of our sensemaking process. The use of stories and the emotions they contain provides a rich vein of insight for the coach to explore in supporting the coachee to gain access to and a deeper sense of self. The coaching space provides a haven where the constraints of society and coherence to its norms are set aside momentarily to engage fully with our stories, their accompanying emotions and what they reveal to us about our public as well as private selves.

As I said earlier, stories also mobilize emotions that are crucial in creating shared values necessary for establishing an organizational culture. This is supported by Barker and Gower (2010), who propose that stories create a sense of empathy which facilitates an understanding of the experiences of others and gain insight into their view of the world. Organizational stories strengthen the culture of the organization by revealing the values and beliefs of the organization and what it perceives its strengths to be. Culture, whether it is social or organizational, is more than rules and regulations that govern that particular culture, instead it is also about the dialogue between the inhabitants of that particular culture. As we will see in the next chapter, through ongoing dialogue the culture continuously evolves and is constructed as a result of ongoing dialogue between participants. It is also through the telling of stories that the organizational myths are perpetuated and kept alive, which may serve as the bonds that keep individuals and the organization together (James and Minnis, 2004). James and Minnis (2004: 28) draw on the three pillars of persuasion as put forward by Aristotle, namely (1) *logos*, which appeals to the intellect, (2) *pathos*, which appeals to the emotions, and (3) *ethos*, which reflects the credibility of the persuader. Emotions have the power to influence the intellect and as emotions are more aligned to physiological responses they are more likely to lead to action. Managers who focus exclusively on the cognitive skills of thinking and analysing overlook the power of emotions in the art of persuasion. Instead, managers who use stories are able to access the hidden, non-rational elements of motivation as it draws on relational as opposed to position power (James and Minnis, 2004).

History is peppered with examples of leaders who have wielded the power of storytelling. Whether for good or evil, they engaged the emotions of their audience for the purpose of persuasion, the result being that they willingly followed and supported the particular vision of the leader. Steve Jobs, the late leader of Apple, is an example of a business leader who had the ability to build an iconic brand through the art of persuasion and seductive storytelling. According to Boudens (2005), the use of narratives and stories provides us with a much richer account of our experiences than a literal description of the same event. Boudens (2005) goes on to suggest that whereas language describes a situation in a linear form, emotions occur simultaneously and in a dynamic and interactive way.

Language is therefore inadequate when attempting to describe emotion. Narratives and stories on the other hand allow us to access information and experiences without the constraints and conventions of literal language. Irrespective of our background and education, we all make sense of situations by linking experiences and events through plot and story lines. The more complex the knowledge and information that we try to share with others, the more inadequate logic and analysis become in codifying the information. Tacit knowledge in particular is much more effectively shared through the vehicle of stories. Business principles will be much more inspirational if shared through a story that draws on vivid imagery and drama to describe a future vision for the organization. The following example demonstrates how effective the use of storytelling can be in turning an organization around:

VIGNETTE

At a recent coaching conference the Chief Executive of an NHS Trust shared his experience, together with the executive coach who worked with him and his colleagues, on how he went about turning around the failing Trust that he had been brought in to put back on track. He spent a significant amount of his time going around the organization sharing his story and vision of what he perceived the Trust had the potential of becoming. Not only did he share his own story but he invited others to do the same, which created joint ownership and helped to create a momentum for change. By engaging both the hearts and minds of everyone in the Trust through the sharing of stories, they achieved their vision for the Trust.

Furthermore, stories are valuable tools that will allow the coachee to rehearse possible scenarios related to a given situation they may want to change or influence. This is particularly powerful in shifting the dynamics as well as the responses and interactions within interpersonal relationships. The use of stories helps the coachee to identify in particular the complexities and dynamics of relationships within an organizational context, such as power and political gaming, and interpersonal conflicts, to mention only a few. Such conflicts are often hidden from view and it is only through the use of stories and narratives that the complexities of these relationships can be surfaced. As Bruner (2002) suggests, we normally revert to stories when things go awry or we find ourselves in a situation that we need to make sense of. Stories provide us with the vehicle to cope with or come to terms with changes, and as with sensemaking it is a retrospective evaluation of a particular experience.

From the perspective of the coach the use of narratives and stories allows the coach insight into the essence of the experiences relayed by the coachee and the main characters influential in these events. Furthermore, it facilitates the discovery of alternative approaches and ways of moving forward. Stories are normally told from one particular point of view and history is very often the tale told from the view of the victor. The view of history from the perspective of the defeated is often very different. As Bruner (2002) suggests, unmasking one perspective merely serves to reveal another. As we have seen with the exploration of sensemaking, stories do not reflect the truth but merely the truth from the perspective of the narrator. As we have seen in the chapter on philosophy, postmodernist thinkers such as Lyotard argue for the little narratives rather than the metanarrative and, in fact, there never could be one dominant story of any event; different views of the event will unfold a different story and perspective depending on the position of the observer or participant. Stories therefore provide models of the world and an invitation to perceive the world as it is embodied within the story. As suggested in the previous chapter on sensemaking, by talking about their experiences the coachee is able to make sense of these events by hearing their thoughts and exploring different stories with their coach. That was the experience reflected in the exclamation of this coachee, when relating the plots and narratives associated with challenging relationship dynamics in her organization:

VIGNETTE

Of course, I knew that! It is so obvious, but it is only now hearing myself say it that I realize that I knew it all along.

As we have seen above, we come to expect emotions as a crucial element of the telling of stories. We anticipate being frightened, kept in suspense and being surprised. A story without the ability to evoke powerful emotions is not deemed a successful story at all. Weick and Browning (1986) suggest that storytelling combines perceived facts with emotions, ideas, values and norms. Emotions have the power to enhance the depth of meaning revealed through the interpretation of the narratives. This leads me to argue that the personal act of making sense of the coaching experience will have greater meaning if the accompanying emotions are acknowledged. Dealing with emotions is not alien to the coach and these often provide the route into the coaching intervention. Emotions also have the ability to reveal issues faced by the coachee which they may not often be aware of at the conscious level.

STORIES AND CHANGE

Change generates new stories and new stories in turn may result in change. Stories may also act as barriers to change (Brown et al., 2009). Stories are often told and retold about the organizational heroes, often the founders of a particular organization. These stories have the ability to keep the organization locked into a past identity that may no longer be suitable to the organization. New stories then need to be created to capture a new vision for the organization. It is through the telling of stories that we are able to make sense of change and experiment with alternative stories and narratives that reflect the possibilities of new realities. According to Gergen (1991), it is also through narrative and dialogue within our relationships that we create our identities. This concept will be explored in greater depth in the next chapter. Drake (2007) concurs and suggests that although coaching facilitates changes at a behavioural level, narratives and storytelling allow the coachee to access storylines related to their identity. The collaborative process of narrative and storytelling allows us to critically assess prevailing assumptions and meanings. The narrative process allows us to understand the relationship between our identities and the environment in which we find ourselves. Stories are valuable not only because of what we include about ourselves but also what we choose to exclude. This reflects the critical skill of listening, as the coach will listen not only for what is said but also that which the coachee chooses to omit.

We may also at times distort our stories to make them fit with our perceived experiences and identities, and a narrative approach helps the coachee to access these distortions and the filters we apply to our sensemaking processes. The coach can support the coachee to write storylines that are more enabling and which will ultimately lead to changes in their behaviour. For us to sustain changes in behaviours it is necessary to rephrase the storylines we associate with. Consequently, through the sharing of our stories we are able to understand how others make sense of the world and the assumptions that underpin their beliefs. As we discussed in the previous chapter, Weick suggests that it is through our stories that we make sense of ourselves and our past retrospectively. They also allow us to negotiate our identities in the present and furthermore how we will enact our envisioned future selves.

Drake (2007: 285) suggests that stories represent five important elements in sustaining identity and which are valuable to coaches in helping them to work with the stories presented by the coachees. These are:

1. Who am I?
2. To whom do I belong?
3. What is my role and purpose here?
4. Why are things the way they are and why do I do what I do?
5. How do I decide what is right, what is important?

As we will see in the next chapter, identity is a dynamic process of continual negotiation between ourselves and our environment and made visible through our stories and narratives. Stories therefore help us to shape our own identities. Working with narratives in coaching allows the coachee to understand how their dominant narratives prevent them from exploring alternative narratives. As Drake (2007: 287) suggests, 'In many ways, we cannot see that which we cannot narrate.' Our existing narratives and stories are an accumulation of the historical narratives from our cultural environments which we have internalized. Coaching provides the vehicle through which we can experiment with new storylines possibly better suited to current and future identities.

As we have seen in the chapter on the prerequisites of coaching, the trust between the coach and the coachee allows for the dialogue necessary to help the coachee to both explore existing stories and experiment in a safe environment with how alternative stories may be more congruent with their evolving identity. Working with stories and narratives in coaching allows the coach to move beyond transactional techniques to a more transformational and dynamic approach. Such an approach would include working with the wider stories in which the individual stories are embedded, such as cultural background, community, gender and organizational stories (Drake, 2007). Within our social communities we create the conventions and implicit framework of language, behaviour and symbols which will connect the members of that particular community and determine the establishment of a group identity, which may to some degree be constraining on the identity of the individual.

The stories of a particular community which are relayed from generation to generation form the invisible threads that keep the community together. Kadembo (2012: 224) argues that stories permeate every aspect of being human: 'the core of humanity is an accumulation of stories; be it in the clan profile, education system, national heritages, inventions, product development, business processes, histories of persons, places, nations, sports and any other entity.' Stories are therefore pervasive, filling every aspect of our lives. Boje (1991) uses the phrase 'terse telling' as representing the idea that the greater the shared understanding of a particular story, the more succinct the telling becomes, creating a code amongst the community which reinforces its identity. Abbreviated phrases and even single words will convey a shared meaning amongst the members of the community created through the layering of storytelling.

The use of stories is not a panacea for organizational leaders but there is significant evidence to suggest that they are a powerful force in influencing the culture of an organization. As we have seen from earlier discussions, they have the ability to influence behavioural changes by working at both the cognitive and emotional levels, which goes on to inspire commitment. The essence of a powerful story is that it allows managers to effectively communicate complex ideas in a way that means people can quickly and easily relate to it. Knowledge and information then become memorable, understandable and relevant to the audience. Examples of stories can include personal experience, case studies and simulations. Kadembo (2012: 228) eloquently defines stories as follows: 'It is my view that stories are the strands by which the web of life is constructed.'

The application of storytelling is a familiar practice within a therapeutic environment and is therefore not a new concept (Parker, 2006). Land (2007: 380) identifies 11 motives for the use of storytelling in therapy, which are equally of potential value to the coach:

1. To direct a client's attention. The story is entertaining and helps to quiet the listener's mind.
2. To make or illustrate a point. Behaviour driven by depression or anxiety can be redefined as a normal part of a process.
3. To set a reflective mood. The story is captivating and helps the client think things over and has healing value because the unconscious mind is learning.
4. To help people recognize themselves. Everyone has had challenges in relationships. Some part of any listener will identify with the action in the story, and, it is hoped, the outcome.
5. To seed ideas and increase motivation. Finding courage is a challenge, but without effort there will be no courage.
6. To redefine a problem. The client starts out fearful; the story presents a challenge that helps the client to rethink the problem and experience a suitable outcome.
7. To decrease 'resistance'. Telling a story is a very low-key approach and is intended to instruct, not give a particular interpretation. The client is free to accept or reject at a metaphorical level anything he or she wants.
8. To suggest solutions. The story refocuses the client's attention to action he or she can take in a direction of change.

9. To embed directives. In the story, the client takes action, goes for a ride, enjoys the day, and learns something new in order to solve a problem.
10. To provide access for diagnosis. On the basis of the client's situation, the therapist will note how the client responds to the story emotionally and how such responses can be used to help the client.
11. To provide leadership in the therapeutic relationship. Stories are metaphors of leading and learning.

Personal construct psychology as defined by Kelly (1991) perceives the individual to be both narrator and actor in the drama of their own life. Kelly was a psychologist who valued storytelling and at the heart of his personal construct psychology is the idea of life being anticipatory. Stories allow us to experiment with possible futures and the anticipation of what we can become. Kelly makes extensive use of storytelling such as in his use of self characterization sketches. He has inspired many by his use of stories to illustrate the human condition and the way in which they were told rather than any facts or data that the individual might have gathered over the duration of their career. Furthermore, personal construct psychology also suggests that the individual has a personal story which they can recurrently invent and reinvent. In essence the life story of a person is seen as being open-ended until the end. Brendel (2009: 33) carried out a study that researched the value of a storytelling approach in medicine, which suggests that the reflective practice of storytelling can be achieved in different ways, namely: 'The use of reflective journals in these qualitative studies seems to provide a safe space through which individuals may enhance or modify their view of self and their environment.' A coach can very effectively make use of this process to support the coachee in developing reflective practice. Stories have the power to connect people to each other and by listening to the story of others it allows us to enter into the reality of the individual.

The perceived value of engagement with people through storytelling is, according to Reason and Bradbury (2008), the fact that it allows new spaces for communication to emerge in which dialogue and development can flourish. There are also many suggestions as to what makes a good story (Boje, 1991; Gabriel, 1991; Weick, 1995). The aesthetic approach put forward by Taylor et al. (2004: 405) is particularly relevant to the coaching intervention as it is concerned with a specific type of knowledge, namely, 'a knowledge of sensation and feeling'. The human element is central to the experience and therefore the human aspect of the story, bypassing the critical and logical filters we may also apply in making sense of phenomena, intuitively grasping the meaning of the story. A coach will often draw on intuitive insight gained from how and what the coachee presents in the coaching environment.

As I have suggested previously, a central theme in coaching is for the coachee to create greater self-awareness. Hyater-Adams (2011) supports this assertion and suggests that the use of reflective stories allows us to deal with emotional distress, doubts and ideas for personal change. Hyater-Adams (2011: 210) proposes that, as she identifies the process, transformative narratives lead to growth and development, and therefore build emotional intelligence capabilities:

> [they] emerge from real and imagined visual, written and spoken stories [to] become material to use for self-awareness, insight, and visioning, and crystalize into deliberate actions for change.

Through the telling of their story, the coachee becomes aware of who they are by tapping into parts of themselves possibly hitherto hidden from view. As Sparrowe (2005: 420) summarizes, 'individuals interpretively weave a story uniting the disparate events, actions, and motivations of their life experiences – much as novelists enliven their characters through the plot.' The coachee is able to make sense of their environment through the use of stories that also facilitate the experimentation with an alternative past, present and future. In addition, storytelling also allows the coachee to understand how their story is influenced by the many stories of others with whom they are interconnected, for example within an organizational environment that is often of relevance and value to coachees.

LANGUAGE AND THE USE OF WORDS IN THE TELLING OF STORIES

Colville et al. (1999) support the argument put forward by Weick that as rhetoric is always involved in the process of sensemaking the sense that is made is therefore a matter of words and a representation of reality and not reality itself. As Bruner (2002: 6) so powerfully puts it: 'Common sense stoutly holds that the story form is a transparent window on reality, not a cookie cutter imposing a shape on it.' Taylor (1999: 527) postulates, 'we understand and make sense of the world as stories'. We create coherence of the complexities we face through the telling of our stories which enables us to organize events (Becker, 1997; Linde, 1993). We are therefore able to communicate abstract ideas and make behaviours possible by creating shared expectations and interpretation (Conle, 2000; Hansen and Kahnweiler, 1993). From a narrative paradigm people come to know what they know by telling stories of personal experiences in different settings. The power of telling one's story allows us to create meaning from our experiences of the phenomena we engage in within the world. It is through our stories that we provide structure to our experiences thereby creating our reality. Brendel (2009: 3) suggests that narratives play a significant role in our learning experiences: 'narratives have been championed as meaning-making devices by preeminent adult learning scholars and introduce studies that support the notion of utilizing narratives as a lever for transformative learning.' As we will see in Chapter 8, which explores adult learning, one of the oldest forms of learning was through the telling of stories or narratives that act as a conduit to knowledge. Brendel (2009) supports the assumption that narrative is a personal account or story that brings meaning to bear on a given situation. Bruner (1991) argues that it is underpinned by a key assumption that reality is constructed as a story that we as social actors are constantly rewriting through a collective process. It is through the construction and reconstruction of our stories that we reinvent our past and our future, and as Bruner (1991: 93) states, 'memory and imagination fuse in the process'.

Berger and Luckmann (1991) propose that language provides the vehicle through which the individual is able to categorize their experiences and assign meaning to them, not only for them, but also for those with whom they engage through numerous relationships. 'The way language is structured therefore determines the way that experience and consciousness are structured' (Burr, 1995: 35). A significant factor that is as important and multi-layered as the language itself is the context within which language is employed. Gergen and Gergen (2008) concur with this argument and challenge the presumption that language has the ability to map the world of human behaviour. Instead they suggest that language is the vehicle that allows groups of people to create shared meaning and understanding. Mumby and Clair (1997) contribute to the notion that it is through ongoing action-oriented communication that different social realities are created.

There are different perspectives on the nature of language and Gergen (2001) suggests that one such view is that language is a vehicle that transmits and reflects the truth of the world as it is, reflecting a deep-rooted assumption that language is able to convey truth. However, he challenges this assumption and proposes an alternative perspective, which is that language in itself does not represent any pictures or maps as to what constitutes reality. Instead it achieves meaning through its use and through the exchange within human interactions. Language is the vehicle through which we are able to share our own particular views and perspectives of reality. Gergen (2001) goes on to argue that without a language through which people express their internal states and characteristics, social life as we know it would not exist. Sim (2001) contributes to the debate on meaning and argues that meaning is transitory and constantly evolving. It has no permanence or substance but is in the continuous process of change.

Sim (2001) emphasizes that it is the joint authorship of meaning between the originator and the recipient which is of importance. The words or symbols drawn on by an author in the telling of their story are suspended and only assume meaning when the reader enters into a partnership with the author and assigns meaning to the words through a co-creative act. Text therefore has inherently a multiplicity of meaning and is dependent on the meaning given to it by the co-creative act of author and reader. Furthermore, each reader will assign a particular meaning to the text depending on the unique experience on which they draw in order to do so. Linstead (1994) concurs and adds that the meaning a reader assigns to text is influenced by their engagement with other texts and cultural forms. Narrative also reflects the richness of social life and interaction, particularly symbolic meaning (Gabriel, 2004), expectations and the quality of fantasy (Taylor et al., 2004). These latter are often hidden within the sentences of the stories that are central in gaining an in-depth understanding of the storyteller, their unique experiences and issues.

NARRATIVES AND POSTMODERNISM

Throughout this book I argue for the importance of a coach to understand the philosophy that underpins their practice of coaching, which, in my opinion, allows them to transcend the obsession with adding the next tool or technique to their repertoire. A philosophy that is associated with our understanding of narrative is that of postmodernism. Postmodernism is an intellectual movement and we can trace its beginnings within the arts and architecture, literature and cultural studies (Burr, 1995). As I introduced in Chapter 3 on philosophy, in essence postmodernism rejects the idea that an ultimate *truth* is possible and that the world as we experience it is as a result of hidden structures. As we have seen, such a truth is labelled as a metanarrative or grand narrative which is seen as the oppressive force of authoritarianism. From his postmodernist perspective François Lyotard (1979) challenges the prediction and control which he perceives as the purpose of a grand narrative and invites us to consider multiple, or *little*, narratives. Truth is therefore characterized by multiplicity and endless variety.

On the other hand, the preceding era of modernity is associated with the need to create order out of chaos whereas postmodernism does not view chaos as a predicament or paradox that has to be conquered, but instead as a reflection of the heterogeneity of the cosmos. Postmodernist knowledge argues for the importance of differences and the tolerance of the incommensurable. Whereas the modernist philosophy is for the search of an ultimate truth or knowledge, the postmodernist approach is towards a polysemic model of knowledge. Postmodernist thinkers argue that today it is no longer trusted nor believed that governments, economic planners or scientists are able to create a better world for the future (Gergen, 1999). This sentiment is particularly relevant in the aftermath of the demise of the banking sector.

Postmodernism is a style of thinking that is sensitive to the complexity of the phenomena under consideration and which encourages the generation of novel ideas through little narratives, which is also true of the coaching intervention. According to Gabriel (2000), postmodernism sees stories everywhere. In order to create a meaningful universe we resort to the telling of stories. Not only do stories create meaning to our experiences, but they also connect us to each other; the glue which holds our various communities together by creating shared assumptions, meanings and values. Not only do stories create our experiences, but experience leads to stories (Gabriel, 2000). Gabriel (2000: 19) goes on to conclude that 'postmodernist discourses have privileged stories and storytelling as sensemaking devices'.

Traditionally, knowledge is considered to be what is stored in tangible renderings such as books, journals, etc. However, postmodernism argues that such renderings are the creations of social interactions. Knowledge is not the property of one individual, it is instead an activity that people engage in together. Wittgenstein in Edmonds and Eidinow (2001) perceives words as the pieces used in a game of chess. Within the game of chess these pieces assume a certain meaning which is dependent on a shared acceptance of the rules of the game and how to use these pieces. Outside the game of chess the meaning would be different. So it is with words; we use words in the same way and engage in a game of creating meaning where the participants know the rules (Wittgenstein, 2001). A postmodernist understanding of language reflects the epistemological belief that the world is constituted and created through a shared language. The difference in meaning from language to language will therefore reflect a different perception or version of the world (Hassard, 1994) and which is equally as valid. Meaning is assigned to each word, which when combined form sentences. Sentences are therefore a complex and subtle array of meanings that constitute the beliefs and assumptions of a certain group of people. As language evolves, so does an understanding of what constitutes the truth of the world or of a particular phenomenon. In fact, Bohm (1996) suggests that shared meaning is the glue that holds communities together. That is also true of professional communities and we have seen over the years how the language and associated meaning of what constitutes coaching has evolved and will continue to evolve. It is fascinating to see how language has evolved over recent years and in particular the influence technology has had on the meaning of language and words. New words and phrases have emerged such as e-mail, the web, social media, facetime, the cloud and so forth, words that would have had different meanings or would not have existed at all 30 years or so ago.

THE DARK SIDE OF STORYTELLING

It is, however, necessary for the coach to consider the darker side to storytelling. Numerous authors perceive storytelling as having the capacity to be used to exert power, manipulate, distort and abuse (Gabriel, 2004; Lapp and Carr, 2008). The research conducted by Boje (1991) reveals that organizational stories may very well be applied in such a manner. An organizational or political leader, through their skills as a storyteller, can evoke emotions through their stories which may manipulate and control their followers. Through our research we consider the possible power dynamics between coach, coachee and the organization for the purpose of selling their stories to one another (Reissner and du Toit, 2011). We propose that each of these stakeholders attempts to realize their own possible hidden agenda by seeking to persuade and even manipulate the others in order to achieve this. This supports the argument of Gabriel (2000) that good stories convince, seduce and have the power to sway others to our way of thinking. As a result of our research (Reissner and du Toit, 2011: 248), we proposed a four-stage model in which (1) the coach sells their services to the organization, (2) the organization convinces the coachee to participate, (3) the coachee engages critically with their stories, rewrites them and (4) disseminates them across the organization to bring about change. In this process, multiple stories interact and inform one another in possibly a constructive or abusive way. There are potentially numerous opportunities for power to be exerted in the complex and dynamic relationship of coaching. One example is between the coach and the coachee, with the latter conferring the status of expert on the coach. The coach may inadvertently succumb to the temptation of stepping into the perceived role as expert and who therefore has superior knowledge and power over that of the coachee. As Linstead (2004) suggests, human relationships are open to the influence of power, perceived or otherwise. The development of a management style that includes coaching makes it a target for the pursuit of self-interest, exploitation and the exercise of power over others.

Therefore, continuing with the underlying philosophy of critical thinking of this text, it is appropriate to introduce a cautionary note in the way we may approach storytelling as a tool in coaching. I draw on the suggestions offered by Gabriel (2004) and quoted by Carr and Ann (2011) that we must be sceptical of accepting all stories as being of equal value and worthy of attention. Instead, as coaches we need to interrogate the stories of our coachees for possible blindspots, illusions and self-deceptions and the exploration of possible alternative stories. In Chapter 4, which explored the prerequisites to coaching, I alerted the reader to the notion of 'story-selling' as being an element of the possible darker side of the coaching relationship. The constructing of and relaying of stories may often be for the purpose of convincing the listener to accept the pearls of wisdom contained within a particular story (Carr and Ann, 2011). It is therefore necessary for us as coaches to explore the motivation of our own stories as well as those of our coachees.

This is particularly the case if we consider that one of the motivations for a coachee in seeking coaching is to obtain the help and support from the coach. This may place the coachee in a vulnerable position as their psychological state might lead them to more willingly trust the value of the stories relayed by the coach. The use of narratives is value laden, and as Carr and Ann (2011) suggest, it is imperative to maintain the reflexivity of storytelling and not to lose its ability to act as a trigger for transformational development. Furthermore, we may also use stories to structure as well as distort our view of how things really are. We can use stories to liberate us from perceived barriers and restrictions but we may also use stories to reinforce limiting beliefs or bigoted views we may hold about others. As we will see from the various aspects of what I have identified as the black box of coaching, the transformative narrative process is interdisciplinary and connects many other fields of study such as visual and written forms of expression, transformative adult learning, management and leadership principles, sensemaking, reflection, dialogue, constructionism, philosophy and psychology to name but a few. I conclude with the wise words proffered by Bruner (1991: 107):

> Narrative, we are finally coming to realize, is indeed serious business – whether in law, in literature, or in life. Serious, yes, and something else as well. There is surely no other use of mind that gives such delights while at the same time posing such perils.

CONSTRUCTIONISM

7

CHAPTER OBJECTIVES

- Define constructionism and its roots within postmodernism
- The contribution of constructionism and reality
- Constructionism as a coaching tool
- Complexity theory and the management of ambiguity

INTRODUCTION

Continuing the theme of postmodernism introduced in Chapter 3 and the discussion on the nature of truth and reality, a constructionist paradigm contests the idea that there is a reality that exists external to us and our particular experiences and therefore the existence of an objective knowledge. Instead, an appreciation of the world is seen as being dependent on an understanding of how we as individuals shape the world internally. From the social constructionist perspective it is through the social interactions and symbolic frameworks within which we interact that we assemble our social identities. As we will see in the following chapter, the philosophy of constructionism is also a key concept associated with adult learning and the co-constructive relationship between the educator and learner. In the same way I will suggest in this chapter it is true of coaching and the relationship between the coach and coachee.

As we have seen in the previous chapter on storytelling, the telling of stories gives us insight into the richness of social life and its interactions, particularly that of symbolic meaning (Gabriel, 2004), expectations, and the quality of fantasy (Taylor et al., 2004). These issues are often hidden within the sentences of the story of a person but tend to be central in gaining an in-depth understanding of the individual, their experiences and issues. I introduced the notion of language as a vehicle through which we transmit and reflect the truth of the world as it is, a belief that carries with it a deep-rooted assumption that language is able to convey an external truth. However, Gergen (1991) strongly argues against this notion and states that language in itself does not represent any pictures or maps as to what constitutes reality; it only achieves meaning through its use and the exchange that takes place within human interactions. Furthermore, he argues that language allows us to express our internal states and characteristics which contributes to shaping the social lives we inhabit. A fundamental belief of constructionism is that the meaning and reality we experience is transitory and constantly evolving and changing without permanence or substance. Sim (2001) emphasizes the joint authorship of meaning between the communicator and the recipient; meaning is dependent on the contribution of both parties. Words or symbols created by an author are suspended and only assume meaning when the reader engages in the co-creative act of assigning meaning to the words. The text therefore has inherent in it a multiplicity of meaning, and different readers will assign different meanings to the same words. Furthermore, our knowledge and awareness of other texts and cultural forms we have engaged with previously will influence the meaning we ascribe to new texts we may engage with (Linstead, 1994).

Reflecting on the nature of constructionism, Gergen (1994: 242) suggests that '[c]onstructionism is one of the more challenging outcomes of postmodern thought'. It is a discourse about the world not a map reflecting what is out there; it is the product of a communal interchange (Gergen, 1985). Individual renditions of truth and reality are perceived as being constructed between people within relationships. Each of the different socially constructed perspectives of the world requires a related action. As our perspectives of the world change, so do our corresponding actions. The objective of constructionism is to invite new forms of enquiry. As with postmodernism, social constructionism does not claim, nor does it offer, a replacement metanarrative of reality and it therefore perceives opposing views as part of the rich tapestry of what is perceived as reality. In keeping with a postmodernist perspective, social constructionism challenges the taken-for-granted beliefs about the world and the perception that our knowledge of the world is acquired through our observations and interactions with others. Reality as we experience it is therefore the result of active interchange between people engaged in reciprocal relationships. As Gergen (1994: 96) proposes, the emphasis is on 'communal interdependence' and collectively we create reality.

Constructionism advocates that there is a multiplicity of ways in which we may construct and interpret the world and rejects any attempt at establishing universal first principles. As discussed in the previous chapter on storytelling, through stories cultures create the norms and rules that determine the assumptions and subsequent human activity which is in keeping with the particular culture, irrespective of whether we refer to a social or organizational culture. These rules reflect the truth the community lives by which constantly evolves with the community itself. These rules are therefore culture-specific and would vary from culture to culture. A constructionist perspective is therefore tolerant of the fact that different cultures will construct a world that differs from the reality of another and will include possible alternative conceptions of reality, knowledge and human functioning (Gergen, 1994). This is a challenge to the consequence of reality becoming objectified, which often leads to closure of arguments, dismissing options, freezing relationships and the exclusion of different voices (Gergen, 1997). As one coachee testifies, it may be difficult to accept that there are different ways of doing things as we have a tendency to revert back to the familiar:

VIGNETTE

You need help to see that there is another equally valuable way of looking at it, which may initially cut across what you think is right or wrong or more valuable, but when you keep probing, and coaching can help you do this, you discover that OK maybe there is another way forward.

According to constructionism, knowledge and truth are seen as evermore being open to redefinition and interpretation. Equally, as we have seen in the chapter on sensemaking, the interpretation of events is open to infinite interpretation and modification.

Furthermore, future events will also influence the interpretative process of current events retrospectively and with hindsight current events may assume very different meanings.

Critics of social constructionism see the concepts as annihilating truth, objectivity, science and morality. However, constructionism enables the reconstitution of the past in far more promising ways (Gergen, 1999). The traditional method of reporting and researching in the human sciences has historically focused on looking backwards. However, due to the dynamic nature of the world, such information is often outdated by the time it is reported upon. On the other hand, a social constructionist approach to research facilitates an understanding from multiple perspectives and multiple walks of life. Instead it encourages dialogue, which also provides ongoing reflection on the reality experienced at a given time, and not merely to reflect on a past but also to create a future.

If we accept that we live in a world that is socially constructed, it is necessary to consider the sources of construction. The media, for example, plays a crucial and significant role in the creation of the reality we experience. The media permeates and saturates everyday life, stimulating desires, creating values and generates ideals and a sense of personal identity (Gergen, 1999). The language used, as well as the images portrayed, infiltrate our thinking and influence the reality society consequently creates and lives. From a constructionist perspective, as soon as we begin to articulate what is objective, or not, what is real or not, we enter the world of discourse and 'thus a tradition, a way of life, and a set of value preferences' (Gergen, 1999: 222). The question as to whether there is a real world out there reflects the Western reality of dualism; a separation between a world *out there* and a world *in here*. As soon as we identify something as being real, from that moment on we exclude other possibilities which may have an equal status in terms of how we define reality.

HEALTH AND CONSTRUCTIONISM

Bruner (1990) supports the challenges Gergen put to the medical profession in perpetuating stories that create ill health in society. The medical profession ignores the power of the stories patients tell themselves in relation to their symptoms, physical or mental, in determining the outcome of their illnesses. These stories will determine the success or not of their recovery. As Bruner (1991: 106) quotes one physician, 'A life is not a record on a chart.' Gergen (1994) has written extensively on the subject of mental illness, illustrating how the understanding of a community as to what constitutes mental illness influences how the *reality* of it is socially and culturally created by the members of the community. According to current definitions of mental deficiency, the assumption is that the person is suffering from a deficit and therefore the victim of an external force over which they have no control. These beliefs are grounded in the strong challenges of Foucault (2006), who equally suggests that mental health is not a scientific fact, but socially constructed instead.

The profession of psychology absorbs and transforms the everyday language of a culture and 'technologizes' it, thereby making it the possession of the profession. The claim to knowledge thereby shifts from the everyday realm to that of a body considered as having superior knowledge, disqualifying the knowledge of the lay person. The common language is devalued and silenced thereby stifling its pragmatic potential. Yet professionals, such as mental health professionals, rely on cultural beliefs for their sustenance. The profession disseminates deficits into the culture which get absorbed and incorporated into daily life, such as *stress, depression* and *identity crisis*. Once such terms become part of everyday vocabulary they gain a status when they may otherwise have gone unnoticed. In turn, such knowledge informs future behaviour and beliefs. As Gergen (1994: 158) strongly argues, 'In effect, the culture learns *how to be* mentally ill.' The result is that the reciprocal process of illness creation continues and advances. We therefore need to be conscious of how the language we use to assign labels to our experiences have the potential to influence and oftentimes determine the realities we will come to experience. The role of the coach is to challenge these assumptions and therefore invite the coachee to create a more enabling view of the world and the reality they are experiencing at a particular moment in time.

Social constructionism is therefore concerned with the practical aspect of creating knowledge. The view of constructionism is not what may be construed as truth, but instead what the implication of truth is on cultural life (Gergen and Gergen, 2008).

They further propose that one of the main tenets of constructionism is that knowledge, reason and morality do not reside within the mind of the individual, but within relationships instead. Day and Leitch (2001) add that according to constructionism, truth is an ever-changing landscape that taps into the rich interplay between experience, conceptualization and a communal understanding. Reality and truth therefore emerge as the result of such communal interaction. These sentiments are also evident in personal construct psychology as defined by Kelly (1991), who suggests that the individual is both narrator and actor in the drama of their own life. He also perceives the individual as having a personal story that can be recurrently invented. Colville et al. (1999) argue that as rhetoric is always involved in the process of sensemaking the sense that is made is a matter of words and a representation of reality and not reality itself. As we have seen in the previous chapter, 'we understand and make sense of the world as stories' (Taylor, 1999: 527).

THE CONSTRUCTION OF IDENTITY

The traditional approach to human relations is to perceive it as a by-product of the autonomous individual whereby relations are secondary to the needs of the personal. However, from a constructionist perspective relationships are a precursor to our individual identity or *self* which becomes known only when juxtaposed with others; the social creates the individual (Gergen, 2001). Bruner (1991: 100) concurs: 'that unique identity derives in major part from the stories we tell ourselves to put those fragmentary pieces together.' Constructionism therefore perceives us as improvisers, constructing our pastiche personalities through the co-constructive relationships we engage in with others. Weick (1979) illustrates this by drawing on the example of jazz musicians, who through improvisation create music in the moment, or as he says, contemporaneously create meaning. McAdams (1997: 5) states that 'identity is a life story'. Furthermore, he adds that it is a story that we create throughout our lives from birth to old age. According to McAdams (1997), if we want to know ourselves and to gain insight into the meaning of our lives we must come to know our own stories, the narrative of self.

Self is not a 'prelinguistic given that merely employs language, much as we might employ a tool, but rather it is a product of language' (Kerby, 1991: 4). With the passing of the certainty of self, and the world of truths, the infallibility of an objective world becomes eroded. Gergen (1991) argues that the postmodernist era places all previous beliefs of what we considered as self in jeopardy. Central to all Western traditions is the existence of the individual self and to question such a fundamental belief is to invite a barrage of scorn. Historically, the self has been as a mirror for what is perceived as being *out there*. The traditional view of personality, or self, is that people have their own, individual personality which remains relatively unchanged throughout their life, representing the essence of the individual. However, Hume (1962) points out that there is no logical justification for an enduring identity just as there is none for the connection assumed between cause and effect. There is no evidence that can demonstrate the existence of personality.

The modernist self is composed of a knowable individual which is present in the here and now. Such an individual is not likely to fall prone to sudden bouts of inspiration or be consumed by a great passion. Instead, the modernist being is a rational one, reliable and predictable (Gergen, 1991). The rigorous, detached and objective scientist who discovers the truth of what is out there is also the domain of an individual knower (Gergen, 1999). The truth observed by the detached scientist is open to infinite variations depending on the vocabulary and cultural language used to describe the same phenomenon. Central to the modernist theme of the individual thinker being the centre of knowledge, is the dictum put forward by Descartes – 'I think, therefore, I am.' This is the rock of certainty upon which the modern world approaches things (Cummings, 2002). However, if we entertain the idea that the mind is not an accurate reflector of what is outside of itself and instead makes things up, then the very idea of individual knowledge begins to crumble (Gergen, 1999). It is from the material of everyday life that we create and assemble the self through narration. The stories we tell ourselves about who we are are part of who we become. These stories also hold the possibilities of who we might become. Language tempts us to posit that the author has to exist in order to tell the story: '... an "I" that acts'. However, Kerby (1991: 65) challenges this assumption by suggesting that,'the "I" is an implicate of these practices rather than a cause of them'.

From a postmodern perspective, the self is open to construction and reconstruction with knowledge and understanding seen as a result of direct experiences. As we have seen in the chapter on sensemaking, our preferences and schemas influence what we perceive, which challenges the notion that we are capable of reflecting the world as it is – the *real* rather than the perceived. Shotter (1993) argues that the notion of the self as a self-enclosed being, living a separate life in isolation from others, is an illusion. Instead, Gergen (1991) suggests that historical assumptions about what constitutes the self are the product of a particular culture at a particular time. Referring to the contribution of storytelling to the shaping of identity, Kerby (1991: 1) argues that 'the self is given content, is delineated and embodied, primarily in narrative constructions or stories'. Narratives are not descriptive of reality, but rather stories about possible realities. Narrative is the vehicle through which meaning is created in the moment of telling (Luhman and Boje, 2001).

The significant advancement of technology and the availability of Internet, e-mail, Skype, Facetime (Apple's version of Skype), texting and various social media has significantly increased the number of relationships people engage with as communication with others is made much easier. The time and distance restrictions have been eroded, increasing the potential and frequency of those relationships. Not only is the frequency and number of relationships increased, but also the nature of those relationships. These relationships vary from being direct, face-to-face, to being more remote and indirect (Berger and Luckmann, 1991). Through an increase in relationships comes an increase in selves, resulting in multiple and disparate selves or the pastiche personality as referred to by Gergen. Ellinor and Gerard (1998: 91) posit that 'we are the sum total of our relationships'. Equally, Luhman and Boje (2001: 160) propose that 'the contemporary social actor exists as multiple discourses, or networks of identities'. Each individual comes to harbour latent selves which may, under the right circumstances, find their way to the surface and ultimate expression. The coaching space provides a safe haven in which the coachee is able to explore and make sense of the different selves and to give voice to the sometimes disparate and competing needs of the different selves.

Our sense of self is dependent on the perception others have of us and how that is reflected back to us (Campbell, 2000). In coaching this would be perceived as the mirror of reflection in which the coachee sometimes discovers the hidden aspects of themselves. Modern technology significantly influences the potential of relationships and new patterns of relationships are continually evolving as a result. An increase in relationships means exposure to different knowledge which results in an increase not only in knowing, but also in what is known (Gergen, 1991). We come to know people in terms of their idiosyncrasies, habits and prejudices as a result of the interactions we have with them (Feyerabend, 1987). Different aspects of ourselves will become prominent in the different relationships we engage in, depending on the context and interactions within those relationships. Different facets of my identity will surface when I am present as the coach rather than other facets of my various selves such as my identity as wife, academic, sister and so forth.

With a multiplicity of selves come increased possibilities as to what constitutes truth. As discussed above, technology exposes us to a much wider range of truth represented by different cultures and communities around the world than experienced by the previous generation. Such knowledge is also instantly available and is not dependent on us travelling to different parts of the world in order to be exposed to different versions of truth. What is considered truth demands a sharing of a common understanding of the nature of such a truth and our exposure to an increasing array of relationships means we begin to absorb and express different truths and identities. Anyone who has ever spent time living in a culture different from their own for any length of time will know the difficulties sometimes of readjusting to the culture you have come from. Exposure to different experiences and cultures means that you absorb different values and beliefs which influence what you may consider to be the truth. What we therefore consider as the *true self* is replaced by a number of different actors in our ensemble who play their part given the circumstances and context at a particular moment in time, resulting in fractional relationships. An increase in relationships infiltrates the self with the self of others. As we are exposed to the different identities of others within our expanded relationship sphere, so the potential of selves that may be expressed increases as it opens up a choice of behaviour, roles and identities.

According to the constructionist viewpoint, relatedness precedes individuality (Gergen, 1994) and with the increase of such relatedness comes an increase or multiplicity of potential selves. As Kelly (1955) suggests, we never need to paint ourselves into a corner as we always have choice of response to any situation we find ourselves in. Steier (1991) argues that the self that we experience at any given time is thus as a result of participation with others. The pastiche personality is born, a personality that is able to flex and borrow from multiple selves to suit a particular moment in time, creating a kaleidoscopic self able to adapt to the moment (Gergen, 1991). Multiple selves are only possible within relationships. Identity is formed by social processes, and once it is established, it is maintained and modified by social relations. Certain social structures engender certain identity *types* according to Berger and Luckmann (1991). Furthermore, identities are sustained because of the relationship we are engaged in in creating an interdependence with others.

CONSTRUCTIONISM AND REALITY

Fundamental to a modernist way of thinking about reality is the assumption of things in themselves – an essence. However, the border between what is considered *fact* and *fiction* is blurring. 'Instead, a new genre emerges, neither fact nor fiction, but *faction*' (Gergen, 1991: 116). A constructionist perspective advocates that whatever the nature of reality, there is no single array of words that is able uniquely to portray such a reality. Instead, there are many interpretations as to what constitutes reality. The very act of understanding the nature of something acknowledges the realization that it may be otherwise (Gergen, 1997). A linear view of the world and of organizations in particular is no longer sustainable in the complex nature of society and organizations.

Postmodernism is therefore perceived as more suitable to the ever changing and evolving landscape that epitomizes social and organizational reality. We can perceive people to be in the midst of a dialectical unfolding with the resulting future not visible at the time of engagement. Postmodernism allows for the flexibility and balancing of paradoxes which are needed for new forms to evolve. Terms such as *true, real, rational* and *objective* serve a purpose and can be very useful within certain contexts, especially within organizations and certain modes of operation. The danger, however, is when such terms are extended to other communities and proclaimed as the *truth* leading to the obliteration and subjugation of other cultures and traditions (Gergen, 2001). The purpose of realism is striving for unity and solidarity, whereas constructionism encourages a state of ambiguity and creativity. The future is therefore undetermined and collectively we all contribute to what will become the future state.

Postmodernism is producing not the known but the unknown, and consensus is therefore that it is a horizon that is never reached (Lyotard, 1979). The traditional view of reality holds that what is known is as a result of experimenting and understanding external phenomena and their *true* nature. However, Gergen (1997) argues that knowledge about reality is the sum total of experiences gained of environmental events. Knowledge of the world is therefore not a reflection of an objective world, but rather an understanding of the world as it is experienced (von Glasersfeld, 1984). The truth we experience is intimately bound up with the culture and community in which we find ourselves. In order to make sense of information and experiences, we divide these experiences into categories. However, these named subdivisions are mere abstractions. We assign labels to our experiences for the purpose of understanding and convenience in order to describe what our perceived reality consists of (Bateson, 1972). These labels do not within themselves constitute a reality that exists external to the observer, but are merely reflections of a communal process of sensemaking. In order to understand meaning from individual subjectivity and then on to a collective understanding through language, relationships may be a more sensible starting point as it is through relations that language and therefore meaning is created. Thus, meaning is perceived as a by-product of relatedness (McNamee and Gergen, 1999). McNamee and Gergen (1999) also argue that it is a continuous process of comprehension, negotiation and adjusting within relationships. There is therefore not a conclusion or stoppage but a continuous process of generating meaning.

Within meaning-creating relationships the notion of a lone individual whose world of meaning, understanding and actions takes place in isolation from others, is replaced with deliberations and meaning-creation collectively (Burkitt, 1999).

'Actions are always preceded by other actions, relationships by other relationships, and the individual self by the selves of others' (Burkitt, 1999: 73). Social constructionism facilitates a dialogue from the many voices representing different cultures in an attempt to understand how realities are constructed (Campbell, 2000). The theme of relatedness is fundamental to constructionism as it supports the relatedness of everything. Moreover, such relatedness leads to the central premise of social constructionism, namely that knowledge is a product of this relatedness and constructed between individuals (Campbell, 2000).

THE SOCIAL CONSTRUCTION OF ORGANIZATIONS

The generation of realities within organizations is as important to the wellbeing of the organization as it is within any other community. Organizations equally have to make sense of the ever-shifting sands of *realities* of their particular environment just as any other community has to for their continued existence. At the time of writing the world is in the grip of financial uncertainty, with the economic realities upon which earlier social truths were built now totally discredited. Financial institutions and political parties are struggling to construct and create a new reality which would be better able to serve organizations, communities and society at large. There is a need for changing and reinventing the rules and perceived realities that govern our financial institutions. Many of the assumptions and truths have been found wanting.

Morgan (1997) argues that the way in which organizations are understood is metaphoric. Gergen (1999: 176) adds that, 'They are lived fictions in a world where there is no living beyond fiction.' All institutions, including organizations, are objectified human activities. However, as powerful and large as organizations may appear, they are the result of human construction (Berger and Luckmann, 1991). Constructionism reminds us, and therefore empowers us, to move beyond the current organizational realities we are experiencing thereby discovering and creating new ones better able to serve their stakeholders. In order to create a new economic reality it would probably be necessary for us to first deconstruct the existing assumptions and beliefs upon which our commercial and financial institutions have been built in order to construct a new reality best suited to the needs of society at that moment in time.

As individuals we achieve acceptance within institutions through the roles that are created for us. The institution becomes embodied within an individual through the enactment of such roles. Through role playing, the individual contributes to the objectifying of the institution and participates in creating society (Berger and Luckmann, 1991). Roles are very clearly defined within organizations: those of leaders and those of the workers, and both need the other to stay within role to secure the continued existence of the other. We come to identify ourselves according to the roles we play. Metaphors are powerful in describing or making sense of the organization, which will influence the way in which it is structured and how organizational members are treated and how behaviour is to be conducted. It is worth considering the paradoxical nature of metaphors. On the one hand metaphors provide an image through which to perceive the reality of an organization and on the other hand, focusing on one metaphor creates blindness to other views of reality. Organizations can become imprisoned by the metanarrative associated with a particular metaphor that prevents it from exploring and expressing other metaphors (Shotter, 1993). The historic metaphors that have dominated economic and financial reality over the past 50 years or so no longer serve the best interests of society and new metaphors have to be created if we are to move beyond the economic difficulties experienced at the time of writing (du Toit and Sim, 2010). Organizations are dynamic and their reality is continually being redefined and renegotiated.

CONSTRUCTIONISM AND COMPLEXITY THEORY

A discourse that is well placed to aid the coach in supporting the coachee in managing the ambiguity and uncertainty of the future our clients face is that of the theory of complexity. A core theme of complexity reflects the sentiments of constructionism, namely that we do not inhabit a predictable and rational environment that we are able to control, and instead supports the overriding theme of constructionism which argues for the emergent nature of reality (Whybrow et al., 2012). The term emergence refers to the characteristics we can identify that emerge within a system, following the interactions of the parts that form the system (Cavanagh and Lane, 2012). It is the interaction between the parts, rather than the individual parts, which is the focus of complexity as it will determine how the system evolves. In systems thinking the focus is therefore on the interaction between the different parts rather than on the parts themselves.

What is not helpful to us as coaches, or researchers of coaching, when endeavouring to understand the environment in which our coachees operate is that much of the concepts and theories of organizations and associated activities, such as leadership, management and organizational behaviour, is approached from a linear view of cause and effect with predictable outcomes. This is due to the assumption that theories are capable of describing the various aspects of our world, such as organizations (Cavanagh and Lane, 2012). Instead, Cavanagh and Lane (2012: 79) argue that it is much more useful to perceive the environments in which we and our clients operate as 'a world characterised by a dynamic mix of simple, complex, and chaotic spaces'. This means that our environments are characterized not only by simplicity and predictability, but also by radical unpredictability. One of the most eminent writers of complex adaptive systems, Ralph Stacey, proposes that, 'Instead, I would argue for a reflexive exploration as the most useful way that a coach can work to sustain and develop the capacity for practical judgment which is the hallmark of the expert practitioner' (Stacey, 2012: 91). Throughout his writings, Stacey argues that there is no blueprint or master plan that will allow us to predict the emergent patterns of a particular system. The implication for us as coaches is to reflect on our reflections and interactions with our coachees.

Managerial thinking has always been influenced by scientific discovery. The contribution made by the study of complex dynamic systems was to uncover a fundamental flaw in the analytical method that is inextricably linked with the study and research of organizations. A complex system is not constituted merely by the sum of its components, but also by the intricate relationship between these components. According to the theory of complexity, non-linear feedback networks have the ability to be both stable and unstable. When a system operates at the edge of instability its behaviour is both stable and unstable and also defined as being the edge of chaos (Pascale et al., 2000). It is not seen as an abyss but instead a state or condition that harbingers potential for innovation and change. The science of complexity reinforces the constructionist perspective of reality creation which suggests that it is the result of the interaction between individual members within the system. Human organizations are examples of non-linear feedback systems governed by laws expressed through relationships. The interactions that take place within the relationships determine the behaviours of the individuals, which in turn evokes a response from others connected to the relationships, resulting in a continuous process of adaption of behaviour of both the individuals within the system as well as the system itself.

Such a system of adapting elements is governed by a set of simple rules (Eden and Ackermann, 1998; Stacey, 1996). As with the flocking of birds, the individual birds respond to a few simple rules and to local information and connections. These few rules are also defined as a strange attractor to which a particular system adheres or responds (Cilliers, 1998). An attractor is a particular state or pattern that a system is drawn to or that unfolds over a period of time. We can also perceive an attractor as a magnetic field. Of significance is that the individuals within the system are free to choose how they wish to respond to the interactions and whether to change the rules and scripts that govern their behaviour. The continuous behaviour of responding, adapting and changing to others within the system brings about a continuous process of co-creation between the individuals resulting in the emergence of the system – a new state or condition (Pascale et al., 2000). Emergence, as identified by complex adaptive systems, is the key concept underpinning the challenge to prediction and thus control within systems and which has dominated organizational thinking (Stacey, 2000).

We can therefore argue that the connected individuals which form the organization are accountable for the system that emerges as a result of their individual co-creation. This supports the sentiments of constructionism that reality is an emergent process and as a result of the interaction of the individuals within the system. Emergence is a central theme of the science of complexity and perceives the emergent system as being greater than its parts (Lewin, 1993). In other words, the whole has a grasp of a larger picture that is unavailable to the individual parts. Furthermore, instead of resisting change we come to understand fluctuation and change as part of the very process that creates order and stability. Complexity theory suggests that order emerges naturally because of unpredictable interaction; interaction is the vehicle by which this occurs and unpredictability is the stimulus that promotes novelty (Marion, 1999). Given that individuals within a system are constantly interacting, nothing is ever fixed but instead is in a constant state of becoming. Systems are therefore constantly learning, evolving and adapting. Stacey (1996) posits that the whole universe appears lawful and yet it has freedom of choice. It is worth returning to the example of the recent banking crisis. The interaction within a system that results in a particular reality is not necessarily of a positive nature and merely follows the simple rules of a complex adaptive system. The result in this case of the demise of the banking sector is therefore the product of the interactions of those within the system.

Systems that resist change and are in balance or in an equilibrium state are by their very nature not going anywhere (Bak, 1997). In living systems, equilibrium is equal to death (Kauffman, 1995). The complex state is seen as the border between predictable, periodic behaviour and unpredictable chaos (Bak, 1997). The edge of chaos, also used to define complexity, is where life has enough stability to sustain itself as well as enough creativity to deserve the name of life – new ideas and innovations that are forever challenging the status quo (Waldrop, 1992). Change and transformation are therefore associated with such non-equilibrium conditions and complexity theory suggests that instead of seeking order and prediction, for a human organization to function coherently it is necessary to focus instead on shared understanding of purpose and a set of values. We can draw the conclusion that the future is truly unknowable and that creative futures emerge unpredictably from self-organizing interactions between members of a particular system.

Furthermore, social and biological systems learn from their experiences and adjust their behaviours accordingly. The very nature of emergence is learning and as we will see in the following chapter the sentiment of transformational learning is that it is not an activity that happens in isolation. It is part of the constant flow of adaption, experimentation and co-creation with others. We can therefore define an organization as a shared meaning system capable of learning, changing and evolving over time through the social interaction among its members and between itself and its environment. Unfortunately, as Nonaka and Takeuchi (1995) argue, employees are often seen as information processors, not information creators. Nonaka and Takeuchi (1995) concur with the power of dialogue discussed in the next chapter and suggest that members of the organization create new points of view through dialogue and discussion and part of the co-creative process that results in the emergence of a new reality.

We can think of the social environment consisting of multiple levels of nested complex adaptive systems in which we operate individually and collectively. Every individual is also a member of several systems expressing different identities, as we have seen earlier in relation to the pastiche personality defined by Gergen. Furthermore, the rules that determine the interactions between the individuals within the system are also socially constructed. We determine the expectations and assumptions we have of those who participate in the various systems. So we establish our social norms, traditions and ideologies, which in turn influence the way other systems such as organizations will behave. At each level of complexity, entirely new laws, concepts and generalizations are necessary, requiring inspiration and creativity. As I suggested earlier, organizations focus on controlling uncertainty, but what the science of complexity adds is that it is a world of creative destruction in that irregularity, disorder and difference play a major part and in which equilibrium is death rather than success. When organizations occupy the space for creativity, behaviour is controlled by the process of self-organization itself and no one is in control (Stacey, 1996). However, a deeply ingrained assumption of organizations suggests that to be successful means to be in control. It is an illusion that an organization can be in control of the kind of complex co-evolutionary process that drives all non-linear feedback networks and instead it can only participate in producing emergent patterns.

The study of complexity further reveals the instability of knowledge as a result of the constantly changing reality of the system and the unpredictable nature of the outcome. Complexity theory supports the postmodernist perspective of reality, reiterating that there is no objective reality out there waiting to reveal its secrets. There are no recipes or formulae, no checklists or advice that describe reality. Instead there is only what individuals within a system create through their engagement with others. Therefore the environment remains uncreated until people interact with it. The world of the complex adaptive system is one of becoming. It is in the continuous flow of creativity, of changing and becoming. An important lesson to learn from the study of complex adaptive systems is that it suggests a futility in the need for prediction and suggests that endless possibilities are lost to organizations through a reductionist need of having to focus on one reality or option. Part of the process of prediction is a fixation within organizations of finding the *right way* of doing things, which by its very nature precludes experimentation or trial and error. What complexity theory demonstrates is that the system must be evermore wakeful and questioning of the assumptions that govern behaviour and remain open to learning and adapting to new ways.

CONCLUSION

The implications for coaching in the first instance is when we seek to obtain evidence-based research based on rationality and linearity that seeks to determine clarity, certainty and control, and as Cavanagh and Lane (2012: 80) postulate, invalidating other forms of research as 'woolly, irrational and uncertain'. The purpose of such research is to find the laws that govern the phenomenon in question which will allow for prediction and association and therefore specific action by applying certain models and techniques in certain situations. However, as we have seen, the world we or our clients inhabit is also, and if not more often, unstable and unpredictable and subject to ambiguity and uncertainty. What is required in terms of the coaching intervention is the approach of the system eclectic coach identified by Clutterbuck and Megginson (2011) introduced in the Introduction, which allows for creativity and solutions that reflect the unique set of circumstances faced by the coachee. The concepts put forward in this chapter support the challenge to the perceived need for the emerging profession of coaching to pursue a grand narrative to be controlled by a professional body. Instead, I argue, that if we approach the emerging profession from the notions put forward by complexity theory, our knowledge, understanding and practice of coaching will continue to evolve through the interactions of those involved in the system.

The constructionist model as put forward in this chapter possibly represents the newest and most controversial theoretical model of coaching. What it does is to offer the coach the opportunity to understand what their individual contribution is to the construction of the discourse of coaching. In addition, it helps us to understand the co-creative nature of the coaching relationship. It is within the coaching relationship and the interaction with their coach that the coachee creates and constructs their identity rather than discovering it. The co-constructive relationship between the coach and the coachee results in the emergence of shared meaning. Reflecting the co-constructive nature of sensemaking put forward by Weick, the coach and coachee co-construct the sense they make of the experiences the coachee brings to the coaching relationship.

As Stewart et al. (2008) suggest, the dynamic and interactive nature of coaching requires a flexible theoretical methodology which would allow coaches to respond with different skills and attitudes in answer to the different needs of different clients. This belief supports the notion that the coachee is capable of creating a preferred future. Constructionism identifies coaching as a transformative experience in which clients are encouraged and challenged to explore issues from different perspectives and to create a reality that best serves them at a particular moment in time. Constructionism provides both coach and coachee with the flexibility to deconstruct and reconstruct the reality of the client. Finally, and in my opinion one of the most fundamental contributions to a philosophy of coaching, is that we work with our clients from the premise that they contribute to the reality they are experiencing and therefore have ownership, as well as choice, of maintaining their present reality or to redefine their reality in a way that might be more enabling to them as individuals.

COACHING AND ADULT LEARNING

8

CHAPTER OBJECTIVES

- Define various approaches to adult learning
- Transformational learning and the parallels with transformational coaching
- Constructionism and adult learning
- Transformational adult learning as a framework for coaching

INTRODUCTION

In this chapter I will introduces the assumption that coaching is not only a journey of discovery but also one of learning. As is expected, learning, and adult learning in particular, is defined in numerous ways with different proponents providing varying themes and approaches as to what constitutes learning. One such definition suggests that learning can be understood as bringing about a change in the behaviour of the learner. This is based on the assumption that learning facilitates either the modification of or adds to existing behaviours. Adult learning is seen as complex and multidimensional, involving an understanding of meaning and self-knowledge gained through critical reflection. The approach to learning that I will focus on, namely that of transformational learning, promotes a learning environment in which the learner plays an active role in their own learning. The result is a collaborative partnership between teacher and learner in the process of constructing meaning and knowledge creation. As I have suggested earlier, learning is a social process that makes it a collective activity (Garvey, 2011).

Learning therefore becomes a reciprocal experience for both the learner and teacher. I will put forward the argument in this chapter that this perspective of learning equally reflects what we would expect to experience as part of the coaching process.

The traditional approach to learning defines it as a process whereby the individual gains new knowledge and skills and possibly also a change to attitudes and opinions. However, in recent years learning has increasingly been seen as a social process that takes place in the interaction between people, resulting in the constructionist view of learning. This sentiment is reflected in transformational learning, which perceives it as an internal process where constructs about self and others are questioned, often resulting in inner struggles. Furthermore, adult learning involves values, feelings, ideals and often moral decision-making and the exploring of self-concepts. We can therefore argue that such learning addresses the subjective world of the learner, challenging the taken-for-granted assumptions they may have about the world. The same can be said of the coaching intervention, which also seeks to challenge and explore the assumptions of the coachee for the purpose of constructing more enabling assumptions if existing assumptions are limiting. The theories of transformational, adult learning reflects the ideas of constructionism, sensemaking and storytelling introduced in previous chapters and, as I will go on to suggest, there are many parallels between what is perceived as coaching and that of transformational adult learning. Exploring coaching through a different lens such as the discourse of transformational learning, we can therefore get a different insight and understanding into the process of coaching.

An approach that may well provide a framework for coaching without imposing a limiting narrative is that of adult learning, namely defined as andragogy. A distinction between adult learning and that of pre-adult learning is put forward by Knowles (1980: 43), who defines adult learning as andragogy, 'the art and science of helping adults learn', and which is in contrast with pedagogy, the art and science of helping children learn. As suggested by Cox (2010), andragogy is underpinned by constructivism whereby learners develop new knowledge based on previous understanding. We can identify five assumptions underlying andragogy, which goes on to describe the adult learner as someone who (1) has an independent self-concept and who can direct his or her own learning, (2) has accumulated a reservoir of life experiences that is a rich resource for learning, (3) has learning needs closely related to changing social roles, (4) is problem-centred and interested in immediate application of knowledge and (5) is motivated to learn by internal rather than external factors. I would suggest that the same applies to the coaching experience. Kemp (2008) puts forward a credible argument that all coaching intervention is encompassed within the broad, generic experiential learning process, or the theory of adult learning, and supported by a significant evidence-based body of knowledge. The root theory of andragogy is that of the discipline of adult learning and development which is underpinned by deep reflection and introspection, scrutinizing assumptions for the purpose of creating new insight and awareness.

The book by Gallwey (1974) entitled *The Inner Game of Tennis* is seen by some in the coaching profession as one of the most influential books in recent years on learning and performance. According to Downey (2003), coaching owes much to the book and proposes that the coach works with the capacity of the individual to learn. Downey (2003) goes on to suggest that coaching is about facilitating learning and development within another at the workplace and beyond. Although there is not a single theory of adult learning, transformational learning theory and critical reflection have been applied to adult learning within the coaching context by a number of authors (Gray, 2006). A coachee shared with me their experience of reflection and introspection resulting from coaching as follows:

VIGNETTE

By the second session it dawned on me that it wasn't moving the way I thought it would, but it was moving inward and what I want from this was a little bit more self-exploration and I think it is because of me. Anyway, I feel it is something I have not done throughout my life, I've avoided it, but I think most people do.

Joy-Matthews et al. (2004) suggest that learning can be understood as a change in the behaviour of the learner as learning facilitates a modification or addition to existing behaviours. This notion is supported by Illeris (2004) who suggests that learning is defined as a process whereby the individual gains knowledge and skills and possibly also a change in attitude and opinion. Learning is not an isolated activity which the learner engages in, but instead there is also the influencing relationship with their teacher, facilitator or in the case of coaching, the coach. De Haan and Burger (2005) perceive learning to be reliant on the one-to-one conversation of coaching, which resonates with Garvey et al. (2009) who consider the non-linear coaching and mentoring conversation to result in deep-seated transformation. De Haan and Burger (2005) go further and suggest that the coaching conversations are rich and full and focus on those issues that are of real importance to the coachee. Gibb and Hill (2006) also propose that coaching has become a significant part of the learning and development discourse and, as they point out, the process of knowledge construction within the coaching community is now under way. Whitmore describes coaching as the 'midwife of this transformation in the evolution of mankind' (Kauffman, 2008: 13). Hargrove (1995), one of the earlier proponents of coaching, describes transformational coaching as the process that supports the individual to stretch their abilities by altering the context that limits the way they think.

This sentiment is a thread throughout the literature on transformational adult learning: the altering of the worldview of the learner as an outcome of transformational adult learning. Hargrove (1995) goes on to offer a powerful definition of transformational coaching and suggests that it is 'unleashing the human spirit and helping people learn powerful lessons in personal change as well as expand their capacity for action'. Releasing the human spirit is what Hargrove (1995: 27) sees as the work of transformational coaching. He describes transformational learning as the culmination of three learning loops, as follows:

1. Triple-loop learning: Transforming who people are by creating a shift in people's context or point of view about themselves.

2. Double-loop learning: Fundamentally reshaping the underlying patterns of people's thinking and behaviour so that they are capable of doing different things.
3. Single-loop learning: Helping people embody new skills and capabilities through incremental improvement.

We attribute the theories of single- and double-loop learning to that of Argyris and Schön (1974). Argyris (1976) continued to make significant contributions to the discourse of adult learning. The relationship with the educator or facilitator is pivotal in the process of coaching, which I discussed at length in the previous chapter. Giglio and Urban (1998) suggest that the coaching relationship provides the opportunity for a 'communal interdependence' which supports the sensemaking of both coach and coachee. This reflects a constructionist perspective which advocates that there is a multiplicity of ways in which the world may be constructed and made sense of and rejects any attempt at establishing universal first principles. As we have seen in relation to the coaching relationship, an important distinction is that this relationship is not a telling one, but instead it is perceived as a learning relationship. The role of the coach is not to impart any wisdom to the coachee, but is there to support the coachee in discovering their own wisdom through questioning and the challenging of their assumptions about situations, of others as well as themselves.

One of the few proponents of coaching who associates it with learning is Kemp (2008), who describes coaching as providing a process of learning through which the capacity of the individual to grow is supported. Cox (2006) is another of the few authors who equally note the absence of the link between coaching and learning as defined by the theories of adult learning. She points out that there is very little connection in the academic literature between adult learning and coaching despite the significant synergy between the two discourses. As suggested above, adult learning is seen as complex and multidimensional, involving an understanding of meaning and self-knowledge gained through critical reflection that is what we would expect of the coaching process. As Garvey (2011) suggests, the reflective nature of the learning conversation facilitated by the coach enables the coachee to think new thoughts, review old beliefs, behaviours and practices. Learning in this context is therefore non-linear, allowing the coachee to construct and reconstruct new and existing knowledge.

Fry et al. (1999) posit that one of the most prominent schools of thought as to how learning takes place is that of constructionism and suggests that it involves transformation. I have referred to the concepts of constructionism throughout the book and perceive it as a significant aspect of understanding the coaching journey. It is therefore an approach that supports the underlying philosophy of this book and from which I draw inspiration throughout. It also reflects the idea of framing and reframing previous schemata as a new experience and allowing new knowledge to be integrated into existing frames of reference, also associated with transformational learning. Bruner (1990), one of the most influential constructionists of the last century, puts forward the idea of a spiral curriculum which challenges the student at increasingly higher levels of understanding. He goes on to suggest that ideas such as experiential learning and reflection are rooted in constructionism, both concepts we would expect to form part of the coaching process.

Vygotsky (1978), an influential theorist in the discourse of learning, introduced the idea of Social Development Theory, which suggests that social interaction precedes the development of a learner and which goes on to propose that consciousness and cognition are the end products of socialization and social behaviour. Therefore, the recognition of the social context in the learning journey identifies the value of collaboration, which leads to knowledge as a product of social creation. Furthermore, the process of collaboration thereby facilitates the movement towards higher stages of learning. In addition, the nature of such a collaborative relationship, the purpose of which is to nurture critical reflective learning, is mutual rather than one-way. Such a relationship is open to difference and uncertainty and not tied to inflexible outcomes as each relationship is unique. Brockbank and McGill (1998) argue that it accommodates the questioning of established ideas through dialogue and embraces the value of tacit and personal knowledge within the learner. The reciprocal nature of the relationship described here is equally applicable to the relationship between the coach and coachee. As coach one often reflects on who is coaching whom as the coach gains as much from the coaching relationship as does the coachee; both learn and develop.

Moon (2006) argues that the traditional view of education which perceives the teacher as the transmitter of information placing them in a position of power over that of the learner, continues to dominate. In contrast, the theory put forward by Vygotsky (1978) promotes a learning environment in which students play an active role in their learning; learning as defined by constructionism. They are not therefore passive recipients to the perceived wisdom imparted by the teacher or facilitator. Instead, the underlying assumption of this perspective is that the teacher and student collaborate in the process of constructing meaning. It is a partnership that requires the participation of both parties. In other words, learning therefore becomes a reciprocal experience for the student and teacher. Continuing with a constructionist philosophy, Mezirow (1991) suggests that learning is not merely adding more knowledge, but instead it is also about the transformation of pre-existing knowledge. The latter could equally apply to coaching as the coach would question and challenge the coachee to reflect on their existing knowledge and its assumptions and the influence it may have on their behaviours and response within certain circumstances and relationships. As Fry et al. (1999) suggest, transformational learning leads to a deeper understanding of the subject and a higher order of cognitive development through changes to the underlying schemata associated with the subject.

Robotham (2004) introduces a pragmatic approach to learning and supports the assertion that effective learning is not only the acquisition of new information, but also the application of the knowledge gained. He stresses that it is not the quantitative measurement of what the learner knows that is important, but what the learner is able to do as a result of that knowledge. However, the assumptions underlying the debate on learning tend to focus mainly on the acquisition of knowledge. Drake (2011) proposes there are many ways of knowing as well as many types of knowledge the learner pursues. There is the knowledge which includes the skills and attitudes of a particular subject as well as knowledge as a living and social process. 'From this perspective, knowledge is less about objective observation and more about subjective conversation, less about facts and more about narrative' (Drake, 2011: 145). Furthermore, he suggests that mastery includes the role of uncertainty.

As we have seen from the discussions earlier, a number of proponents of learning argue that the learning journey also leads to a relatively permanent change in behaviour, which occurs as a result of the interaction the learner has with the environment (Billett, 2004; Werner and DeSimone, 2005). Sadler-Smith (2006) concurs and supports the view of learning associated with the development of the learner over the longer term. This view includes therefore the capacity of the individual to lead a more fulfilling life both personally and professionally. We associate the latter position with a developmental perspective of learning and which, as I argued earlier, is an explicit expectation of the coaching intervention. The following demonstrates the awareness of a coachee when they realized the impact coaching had had on their behaviours:

VIGNETTE

The recognition is almost not enough, is it? You need to actually change your behaviours, you need to actually do something and so slowly changing your behaviours and then reinforcing them. Otherwise, you can be as aware as you like, if you're not doing anything differently it is a waste of time.

Senge (1990) goes further and suggests that it is through learning that we re-create ourselves, which resonates with the concepts of constructionism. The ideas of learning have in recent years increasingly led to the perception of learning as a social process that takes place in the interaction between people, resulting in the constructionist view of learning (Burr, 1995; Gergen, 1985, 1991, 1994). Work-based learning, associated with adult learning is, according to Grady (2001) allied with reflection on working practices. He supports the arguments of others which I introduced earlier, namely that work-based learning is not only about the acquisition of new skills, but includes the ability to reflect on experience. The connection between learning and experience was first put forward by Dewey in 1938, who saw all humans as having the ability to learn from experience. He also believed that education was a

lifelong process; a continuous journey until death. This sentiment of learning and education is reflected by other theorists of
learning such as Mezirow (1991), who concurs and argues that
a framework for adult learning has to include the recognition
of how adult learners create meaning out of their experiences
and the dynamics involved in adapting these meanings. Holman
et al. (1997) go further and suggest that experience is the most
important source of learning. We make meaning of these experiences through internal reflection and how they relate to our
existing knowledge. Equally, the coach engages in this process
of reflection with the coachee for the purpose of supporting
their sensemaking of a particular situation or circumstance.

As suggested earlier, building on the theme of constructionism, some proponents of work-based learning perceive learning
as a collective activity. As mentioned above, the argument put
forward is that learning does not take place in isolation, but
instead occurs through debates and the sharing of problems
and solutions. A further significant element of work-based
learning is, according to Gray (2001), the ability of the learner
to develop meta-competence – the ability of the learner to learn
how to learn. It is also a form of learning that relies on experimentation, trial and error. Another significant and crucial
aspect of the learning process suggested by Harrison (2005) is
the ability to unlearn. Learning also includes the ability to learn
what or how not to do something as well as how something
needs to be done. Furthermore, the reliance on personal reflection, dialogue and feedback from colleagues is of equal importance in the learning journey of the adult learner. There are,
however, critics of work-based learning who suggest that it
conceals aspects of power and does not adequately address the
question of whose agenda is being served (Easterby-Smith et al.,
1991; Huzzard, 2004). As I have discussed elsewhere in the
book, the dilemma of whose agenda dominates the coaching
process often poses a challenge to the coach and to which there
is no one easy or simple answer.

Brookfield (1995) challenges what he defines as the myths of
adult learning, which hold that it is inherently joyful, that adults
are innately self-directed learners. Furthermore, that good educational practice always meets the needs articulated by learners
themselves and that there is a uniquely adult learning process

and adult form of practice. Instead, he strongly argues that research into adult learning should also consider the emotional dimensions of learning and how adults learn about their own emotional selves and which are, according to Brookfield (1995), rarely addressed. The role of emotions in learning is also supported by Dirkx (2001), who argues that personally significant and meaningful learning is fundamentally grounded in and derived from the emotional, imaginative connection of the adult with the self and with the broader social world. He goes on to argue that emotions can either impede or provide motivation for learning. However, such emotions are not always of a positive nature, as one coachee shared with me:

VIGNETTE

I think it is always strange with transformational learning that people assume it is very positive and yes it may be very positive in the end, but I think it sometimes requires you to work through something that is painful and to realize that there is light at the end.

Furthermore, Brookfield (1995) proposes that if we are to understand adult learning we also need to explore the processes of meaning-making, critical thinking and entering new cognitive and instrumental domains, which are viscerally experienced processes. He adds to the debate of adult learning and argues that it is a socially constructed phenomenon and concurs with the notion that adult learning is socially embedded. His arguments support the perspective of learning as a socially constructed process argued above.

REFLECTIVE DIALOGUE AND LEARNING

According to Quick and Macik-Frey (2004), personal development is achieved through deep personal communication, and they go on to suggest that it is through the engagement of reflective dialogue with others that we create the conditions for critical reflective learning. The importance of the relationship is once again highlighted by Moon (2006), who argues that this process requires not only a particular kind of relationship between teacher and learners, but also among the learners themselves. The requirement and ability to suspend a personal need to be right and a willingness to embrace different perspectives for the purpose of learning and developing are necessary if dialogue is to be achieved. As far as Senge (1990) is concerned there are a number of conditions necessary to achieve the level of dialogue outlined by Bohm (1996), who wrote extensively on the subject of dialogue and the requirements necessary for participants to engage in dialogue. Of significance is the need for participants to suspend their assumptions and to perceive one another as colleagues, which requires a sense of equality and a shared quest for deeper insight and clarity. Senge (1990) goes on to suggest that hierarchy and power are antithetical to dialogue. Finally, there must be a facilitator who is able to hold the context of dialogue; it is not a state achieved by an individual in isolation. These conditions allow for the free flowing of meaning to pass between the participants, and in the learning context, between the learner and facilitator, which once again reflects the constructionist approach to learning as I put forward above.

De Weerdt (1999) adds to the discussion on dialogue, identifying dimensions of exploration and going on to challenge goal-driven communication; he suggests that it is fixed and permeated with hidden agendas and with an urge to agree on what is 'real'. It can also be argued that such communication is also subject to control from the fixed position of the communicators. Instead De Weerdt (1999) argues that within dialogue the communicators relinquish the need for control in favour of 'space', a concept I referred to in a previous chapter as being associated with coaching. The suggestion that dialogue is a powerful way of making collective sense of our experiences is supported by Dixon (1999), who goes one step further and suggests that dialogue is the most powerful form of communication, allowing us to reveal our meaning structures to ourselves and others.

The underlying principles of the dialogical space reject the idea that texts and words can be interpreted in a single, solid and rational way. Instead it attempts to bypass the obvious and sheds light on interpretations that may otherwise have remained hidden. Dixon (1999) argues that this space embraces divergence, multiplicity and possibility rather than the convergence, uniformity and certainty of direction. Furthermore, within dialogue goals do not precede or dominate interaction, but are construed and continuously modified along the way. Bohm (1996) argues that this becomes possible when people create space that facilitates open-ended interaction.

TRANSFORMATIONAL LEARNING

As we have seen from earlier discussions, Winch and Ingram (2004) support the assumption of transformational learning as inner learning where constructs about self and others are questioned, often resulting in internal struggles between opposing views. As noted above, they also perceive transformational learning to include emotional energy that impacts on how the individual perceives themselves. This was very much the experience of one coachee, who shares his experience as follows:

VIGNETTE

Unlike all of the programmes I have done before there is not an emotional element to it, but with this programme [coaching] there is an emotional element to it and the coaching has made me think about who I am and there is a fundamental desire to change and I don't mean on the surface level.

If we pause for a moment on the definition of transformation, in the *New Shorter Oxford English Dictionary* the word 'trans' is described as meaning 'across', 'beyond' and 'into another state or form'. Through *transformational* learning the individual is therefore deconstructing their formative learning for the purpose of constructing a different and possibly a more inclusive view of the world. Such learning, according to Senge (1990), is the ability to continually clarify and deepen our personal vision by challenging our mental models.

The underlying principle of transformational learning, namely to understand how individuals construct meaning and the theories of transformational learning as postulated by Mezirow (1991), draws on the corollaries of Kelly (1955) and personal construct psychology to enable such understanding. Personal construct psychology suggests that the meaning made of a particular event will in turn guide the expectations of future events and their anticipated meanings. Mezirow (1991) argues that adult learning involves values, feelings, ideals and often moral decision-making and the exploring of self-concepts. Brockbank and McGill (2006) associate such learning with the subjective world of the learner, which goes on to challenge their taken-for-granted assumptions about the world. Lämsä and Sintonen (2006) add to the debate and suggest that transformational learning is the process through which the learner transforms meanings hitherto taken for granted which enables such meaning to be reinterpreted in a wider, more open and reflective manner. As Garvey (2011) suggests, learning leads to personal transformation and the emergence of new possibilities and new perspectives about the world around us. A coachee shared with me the challenge of trying to articulate the transformational experience:

VIGNETTE

The language of that deeper level, as soon as you go beyond behaviours, is perhaps not words, which is why we find it so difficult to articulate that it really is a different type of communication, which is why intuition then is important in terms of sensing things, so it is almost as though one needs a different form of communication that goes beyond behaviours.

Mezirow (1981) put forward 10 phases of meaning in the process of transformational learning:

1. A disorientating dilemma.
2. Self-examination with feelings of shame, fear, guilt or anger.

3. A critical assessment of assumptions.
4. Recognition that one's discontent and the process of transformation are shared.
5. Exploration of options for new roles, relationships and actions.
6. Planning a course of action.
7. Acquiring knowledge and skills for implementing one's plans.
8. Provisional trying of new roles.
9. Building self-confidence and competence in new roles and relationships.
10. Reintegration into one's life on the basis of conditions dictated by one's new perspective.

Although described in a linear way, I suggest the above phases are experienced in a messy and non-linear way. I also suggest that these phases are evident in the coaching process. As with coaching, we can trace the roots of transformative or transformational learning as experienced by the adult learner back to the literature of psychology and philosophy (Cranton, 1994, 1996; Mezirow, 1991). I discussed at length the influence of psychology on coaching in an overview of coaching in Chapter 2. Many of the theories of transformational learning have their roots in the work of Aristotle and more recently that of Habermas (1971), who identified three domains of learning, namely:

- The technical – knowledge is governed by technical rules.
- The practical – based on social norms.
- The emancipatory – self-knowledge and self-reflection.

Mezirow (1981) defines transformational learning as the ability of the learner to make their assumptions explicit and then to act upon them. It is therefore through transformational learning that the learner learns to identify the distorted meaning perspectives they may hold in terms of understanding their own motivations and the motivations of others. Mezirow (1991) also suggests that the individual is governed by meaning schemas which provide the rules that dictate their behaviour. These schemas encompass the specific knowledge, values and beliefs, value judgements, feelings and assumptions the learner has about themselves, others and the world in general. The ability of transformational learning is therefore to enable the learner to critically reflect on these schemas for the purpose of deconstructing existing schemas and reconstructing schemas that are more inclusive to allow changes in behaviours. Mezirow (1997) goes on to suggest that transformative learning develops autonomous thinking – learning to develop the ability to learn, an assumption that is also true of coaching. The latter is supported by Wilson (2007), who states that one of the core principles of coaching is that of self-responsibility and ownership. He goes on to argue that this is possibly due to the confidence we develop within the space provided for learning and experimentation. O'Donoghue and Maguire (2005) postulate that the lifelong learner needs to master the process of learning to learn in order to transfer knowledge and skills into new contexts in the future. The goal of transformational learning is for the learner to go within themselves and to reflect critically on the meanings they hold about the world for the purpose of revision (Cranton, 1994; Mezirow, 1991). Mezirow (1991: 93) puts forward four stages of transformative adult learning:

- *Learning through meaning schemes* – learning to further differentiate and elaborate the previously acquired meaning schemes that we take for granted, or learning within the structure of our acquired frames of reference. This form of learning includes habitual and stereotypic responses to information received through pre-existing, known categories of meaning. The only thing that changes within a meaning scheme is a specific response.
- *Learning new meaning schemes* – creating new meanings that are sufficiently consistent and compatible with existing meaning perspectives to complement them by extending their scope. In this form of learning our meaning perspective does not change fundamentally, even though it is extended.
- *Learning through transformation of meaning schemes* – learning that involves reflection on assumptions. We find that our specific points of view or beliefs have

become dysfunctional and we experience a growing sense of the inadequacy of our old ways of seeing and understanding meaning. This accretion of transformed meaning schemes can lead to a transformation in meaning perspective.

- *Learning through perspective transformation* – becoming aware, through reflection and critique, of specific presuppositions upon which a distorted or incomplete meaning perspective is based and then transforming that perspective through a reorganization of meaning.

This last is the most significant kind of emancipatory learning. It begins when we encounter experiences, often in an emotionally charged situation, that fail to fit our expectations and consequently lack meaning for us, or we encounter an anomaly that cannot be given coherence either by learning within existing schemes or by learning new schemes. Illumination comes only through a redefinition of the problem and redefinition in turn is achieved by critically reassessing the assumptions that support the current meaning schemes in question. A coachee identified the value of emotions in gaining an awareness of his values and beliefs:

VIGNETTE

Certainly what it feels like is that emotions are almost a channel or a vehicle into our values and beliefs and then greater awareness and understanding and that it is actually the facilitator of understanding.

We cannot leave the debate on adult learning without drawing on the notion of actional learning. Adult and work-based learning resonates with the notion of action learning as identified by Pedler and Burgoyne (2008), who argue that it is best understood as a philosophy rather than a set of techniques. They go on to suggest that the action learner has to deal with more than just developing technical skills, but also has to consider issues around values and ethics. Mezirow (1990) concurs and proposes that transformational learning does not happen in isolation and is indeed a social affair that requires interaction, debate, and being exposed to alternative realities. Consistent interaction with others is seen as fundamental to the development of meta-learning (Lizzio and Wilson, 2004). As we have seen from the various arguments put forward, theorists advocating transformational learning (Cranton, 1997; Gray, 2006; Mezirow, 1994) argue that it is developing an awareness of assumptions held about self and others and, more importantly, the ability to critique those premises. We can therefore conclude that the outcome of transformational learning is the emancipation from perceived limited options, which may have acted as a constraining force on the life of the learner. The latter is of equal importance in coaching and has been addressed at length in previous chapters. Changes in behaviours are often an outcome of such emancipation. Learning of this nature is only gained through critical self-reflection as opposed to the technical knowledge acquired through learning and which I argue is equally true of coaching.

THE TRANSFORMATIONAL EDUCATOR

The literature on transformational learning makes numerous references to the importance of the relationship between the transformational learner and facilitator who supports the learning journey of the learner. Pounder (2006) draws a parallel between transformational teachers and transformational leaders and he puts forward the argument that both roles draw on the same set of skills. One of the assumptions he bases this on is the notion that both have a fundamental belief in profound potential. Furthermore, he also posits that an underlying principal of transformational leadership is that it is a process rather than positional. This makes it more difficult to articulate as it embraces a number of characteristics as opposed to specific duties and roles. A number of proponents of the teacher leader have attempted to identify the properties of the ideal exemplar, namely a sound knowledge of pedagogy or andragogy, research-based knowledge of teaching and learning, and effective classroom practices among others (Pounder, 2006; Sherrill, 1999).

Contributing to the debate, Cranton (1994) suggests that the educator can approach their role from one of two different perspectives. In the first instance, the educator who approaches learning from a positivist's perspective sees learning as being subject-specific and their role as being the provider and disseminator of knowledge; the so-called expert in a particular topic in other words. On the other hand, the educator who approaches learning from a constructionist perspective perceives learning as transformational and their role as one of responding to the individual needs of the learner. Learning from this perspective is then perceived as a process for the express purpose of releasing potential and to transform the learner. The educator therefore gets off the centre stage and focuses instead on supporting the learning journey of the learner. Cranton (1994) describes the role of educator in the latter approach as that of facilitator who perceives their role as providing support and encouragement, focusing on the building of trusting relationships of a non-judgemental nature, accepting the learner as they are, including their particular worldview. Cranton (1994) adds another dimension to the role of the transformational educator, namely that of provocateur, encouraging critical thinking, challenging assumptions and norms and stimulating thinking. The principles of transformational learning as put forward by Cranton could also have been written about coaching and the role of the coach in the coaching relationship.

Furthermore, I would add that transformational educators are lifelong learners themselves. In order to support the learner in engaging in transformational learning, they have to experience the process themselves in order to understand the challenges transformational learning poses to the learner. The transformational educator would therefore constantly be engaged in critical thinking and reflection on the assumptions of their practice, themselves and their learners. All the techniques the educator will employ to facilitate transformational learning are equally applicable to their personal lifelong journey as an educator for the purpose of developing, updating and deepening their ability to facilitate transformational learning. If we pause to reflect on what the purpose of transformational learning is, we would want to determine what the learner and the educator hope to achieve at the end of the process? It could be argued that the educator is not a necessary factor in transformational learning, but if we subscribe to a constructionist approach to learning, I would suggest that the educator is an integral part of the social construction of knowledge as argued extensively above.

The very nature of transformational learning, which addresses the psychological, epistemic and sociolinguistic meaning perspectives of the learner, raises the same issues and debates of ethics. The question arises whether the adult educator is engaged in psychotherapy during the process of supporting the learner to challenge their worldview, similar to questions posed of coaching. Mezirow (1991) makes a helpful distinction between adult learners who are undergoing life transitions and those with neurotic, psychotic or sociopathic disorders requiring therapy and treatment. Furthermore, Mezirow (1991) argues that there should be no reason why the adult educator should not act as counsellor or instructor to the healthy learner making decisions about life transitions. The same debates are true of coaching and I referred earlier to the psychological mindedness defined by Bluckert (2005). It is for this reason that the psychological community argues that coaches should have training in psychology or therapy to support the coachee if issues such as these present themselves during coaching. Mezirow (1991) also acknowledges that engaging in such a process requires knowledge and sensitivity as to the psychological processes, but maintains that it is not classified as therapy. One key distinction we can identify between transformational learning and therapy is that the process of transformational learning centres on a specific outcome or purpose, such as career transition or realizing and developing personal potential. Critical transformation in higher education is about people who can produce new knowledge and developing a high self-awareness within the student. Mezirow (1991) also suggests that transformational learning is seen as the process that encourages the learner to become a critical thinker within their discipline. Furthermore, the ability to think critically may also extend to the ability of engaging in critical thought with their peers and colleagues, thereby recognizing the relativity of knowledge.

A further parallel we can draw between the role of the coach and that of the transformational teacher as described by Pounder (2006) is that transformational teachers have a profound belief in potential, which I have also identified elsewhere as being a given of coaching. The view held by Cranton (1994) as to the role of the educator in transformational learning is to perceive the educator as the provider of support and encouragement. The educator's focus is on building a trusting relationship of a non-judgemental nature, accepting the learner as they are, including their particular worldview and one which is equally associated with the coach and which I discussed at length in the previous chapter.

Although tentative reference is made to learning as an outcome of coaching in the literature, it is only explicitly identified as a key component of the coaching intervention by a limited number of theorists (Cox, 2006, 2010; Kemp, 2008; du Toit, 2010). Furthermore, the elements associated with transformational adult learning as discussed above, such as critical reflection and inner learning, are not evidenced in the coaching literature as part of the coaching process. As we have seen, the literature on transformational adult learning makes extensive reference to constructionism as a fundamental aspect of the learning process. Despite the parallels between transformational learning and coaching, there is no reference to the co-constructive relationship between the coach and coachee in the coaching literature. Moreover, the co-constructive relationship between the educator and learner is explicitly associated with the literature on adult transformational learning. The emergence of learning created between the educator and learner or the coach and coachee challenges the assumptions associated with goals and objectives and the need to establish these at the beginning of the coaching relationship. Instead, based on the discussions of transformational adult learning put forward in this chapter, I am particularly drawn to the learning aspect of coaching. I have endeavoured to construct the argument in this chapter which suggests that coaching is intimately linked with the theories of adult learning. This is succinctly described by Cox (2006: 195) as follows:

> I would argue, in fact, that andragogy has reached its zenith with the advent of coaching as a learning approach: Knowles' definition of andragogy in 1980 confirms the birthright; the learner is perceived to be a mature, motivated, voluntary, and equal participant in a learning relationship with a facilitator whose role is to aid the learner in the achievement of his or her primarily self-determined learning objectives.

This statement also reinforces the importance of the relationship between the coach and coachee and which resonates with the constructionist position of transformational learning discussed above. It may very well be that andragogy, as discussed in this chapter by the various proponents of adult learning, could provide the emerging profession of coaching with an overarching philosophy. Furthermore, it may do so without imposing a rigid framework on coaching, recognizing that each learner and learning environment will be different (Brockbank and McGill, 2006; Cox, 2006; Kemp, 2008). This assumption supports my personal challenge against the need for regulation and the imposition of accreditation. Although I understand the motivation for introducing accreditation and the exclusion of those who are not perceived to be suitably equipped with the necessary skills and competencies as a coach, on the other hand I argue that it enforces conformity and the perception that all learners are the same with similar needs and expectations of coaching. Instead, as we have seen from the debates on adult learning, each coaching relationship is a unique construction between the coach and the coachee, further complicated by the influence of the organization and/or various stakeholder groups. It is for this reason that it is so difficult to define the nature of coaching.

CONCLUSION

The purpose of this book was to develop our understanding of the black box of coaching through the use of the heuristic I introduced in Chapter 1. As Hodge (2012) suggests, a heuristic captures the key themes of a discourse without providing universal laws. In fact, the main theme throughout this book was to constantly remind us, author and reader, of the potential pitfalls of establishing so called universal first principles, or a metanarrative, of coaching. Instead, I have argued that in order to get closer to what we might perceive coaching to be and contribute to supporting its ongoing evolution, it is necessary for all with an interest and stake in coaching to engage in conversations and dialogue that include divergent views, offering multiple approaches and solutions. I reflect on the advice of Cavanagh and Lane (2012: 127), which suggests, 'Furthermore, ongoing iterative engagement in such conversations is more likely to lead to (but again not determine) creative outcomes.'

Throughout this book I have argued that one of the most important elements of the development of the coach is to determine what their personal philosophy is which will underpin their practice. I have singled out critical theory as one example, discussing how it could both challenge and support the understanding of coaching and its practice. The benefit of critical theory is that it provides a framework for us to question the motivations and assumptions of the various aspects of coaching. Having a philosophical position is not only of importance to the individual coach, but also to the emerging profession as a whole. Engaging in philosophical discussions about the nature of coaching and how it is to evolve will support conscious decisions as to the future of coaching and contain the personal agendas of different groups vying for ownership of the regulation of coaching. As we have seen, from a theoretical perspective coaching is in its infancy and is informed and influenced by numerous divergent discourses. Each of these have made their own contributions as to what constitutes coaching. Irrespective of the different approaches or routes taken to coaching, the common theme is that the purpose of coaching is for the growth and development of the coachee. There are also assumptions as to what we would expect to see as outcomes of the coaching intervention as the final stage of the proposed heuristic and which I discuss below.

In this book we have journeyed through the heuristic which I propose give us an insight into the black box of coaching. This journey has included a discussion of the prerequisites of coaching, which make a significant contribution to the eventual successful outcome of the coaching intervention. I have then introduced what I perceive to be the mainstay of what transpires during the coaching intervention, namely for the coach and coachee to make sense of what the coachee brings to the coaching relationship. They achieve this through the sharing of stories and together construct meaning in the situation by engaging in dialogue. Throughout the text the various discourses introduced, such as postmodernism, constructionism and complex adaptive systems, support the overriding theme of postmodernism, which suggests that there is not only one way or truth associated with a particular situation or circumstance and therefore it is always open to reinterpretation and redefinition. Coupled with this philosophy is also the message that we are not victims of circumstances, but in some way contribute to the reality we experience. This is a liberating and emancipatory message which suggests that we are able to recreate our reality to one that is more enabling, should we choose to do so. In the spirit of storytelling, we can write a new and different story.

One of the key outcomes of coaching is to provide the coachee with the tools to self-coach and to prepare the coachee to be more self-directed in their own learning. This process will include a greater sense of self-awareness and the potential for further growth and development (Moen and Federici, 2012). Self-efficacy is also perceived as an outcome of coaching, which enhances the self-belief of the coachee that they have the ability to achieve the outcomes and tasks expected of them. Self-efficacy is also associated with resilience within the individual and is accompanied by a mastery that is able to identify the level and quality of skills the individual employs in executing a particular task. A further element associated with self-efficacy is the perceived level of control the individual has over their environment and their personal contributions (Weiner, 1985). The latter is supported by Strauss et al. (2008), who suggest that an increased level of self-efficacy leads to personal control and the belief within the individual that they have the capacity to be successful. Furthermore, self-efficacy is accompanied by a personal belief and confidence within the individual in their abilities. One of the key factors that enhances performance is heightened self-awareness. This includes a know-how of the factors that influence individual performance and the knowledge and mastery of how to take control of these and make the necessary changes. Research conducted by Moen and Federici (2012) on a group of executives suggests that coaching is a successful tool in developing the capacity for personal change in individuals.

OPPORTUNITY FOR REFLECTION

My own experience and the stories others have shared with me about their experiences of coaching would suggest that one of the overriding benefits of coaching is that of reflection. One senior leader shared his experience with me following a leadership programme which included the support of coaching:

VIGNETTE

The most effective part of coaching for me is the reflection, thinking about things and also having some help with that reflection. The coach helps you to focus on what is relevant and what isn't relevant. I think personally the reflection has been a really big thing because before the programme and the coaching I would say I was really good at reflecting, whereas really I think I was probably good at stewing. I think that coaching is the way of unlocking the potential in people.

According to Brockbank and McGill (2006), reflection is the precursor for improvement and transformation. Kilburg (2002) proposes that the coaching environment provides a structure within which the coachee can safely explore specific aspects of their life. As I have discussed in an earlier chapter, the coaching space is seen as facilitating and enhancing the quality and depth of such reflection. Proponents of transformative learning perceive the ability for reflection as a key component (Gunnlaugson, 2007). Associated with reflection, as Gunnlaugson (2007) identifies, is the co-constructive nature of dialogue. This process of reflection and dialogues allows the coachee the time to talk about things that affect them and provides the opportunity to work through these issues with someone with whom they have built a trusting relationship.

As we have seen from earlier chapters, transformational coaching is about what is deep and meaningful to the individual, reflecting on what lies beneath the behaviours – the values and beliefs. This is partly due to the fact that coaching challenges the coachee to think more deeply about why they do what they do and challenge their frames of reference. The transforming of a worldview held by an individual requires the ability of that individual to reflect on their assumptions and beliefs. Tennant (2005) suggests that for personal change to occur, it is necessary for the individual to engage in exploration of self, achieved through the use of different methods such as reflection and contemplation. Mezirow (1991) refers to this as critical self-reflection and Dirkx (2001) describes it as 'soul work'.

Moore (2005) points out that transformational learning requires the ability of the individual to reflectively transform attitudes, opinions, beliefs and emotional reactions which constitute their meaning scheme. It is necessary to point out that as Moore (2005) suggests, this journey may very well be painful or uncomfortable at times. However, the coach acts as a companion to share it with, someone who can reflect the comments of the coachee back to them. The same is true of transformative learning, and according to Mezirow (1990), it does not happen in isolation. It is instead a social affair that requires interaction, debate and being exposed to alternative realities. The notion of reflection can be seen as the same way that a mirror reflects images back to the observer, as the following coach suggests from her own experiences:

> ## VIGNETTE
>
> I was really surprised at how strong that was. People don't listen to what they're saying, they just say things. So to listen to what you say and have somebody else listen to everything, but then just giving sharp points of reflection back again. If the coach wasn't there and it was just a personal self-reflective moment I don't think you can go as deeply into your own thoughts as somebody else can that is listening, you don't verbalize it, it stays internal. I think the coaching makes both parties think inward because deep listening does not just happen on the surface, you draw it into yourself.

Furthermore, there appears to be a general consensus that the process of reflection continues beyond the coaching sessions themselves, facilitating the ability of the coachee to become much more reflective in other situations and circumstances, standing back from experiences and questioning the consequences of possible actions. The power of the coaching conversation is in creating the ability to reflect much deeper than the coachee could have done on their own, which reflects the assumptions of transformational learning discussed earlier in the previous chapter. As Rogers (1980) points out, the greater the self-awareness an individual has the greater the chance that more informed choices will be made. Reflecting on the key criteria of dialogue as discussed in Chapter 8 it is apparent that it transcends what is understood as conversation. As we have seen, proponents of dialogue suggest that it contains dimensions of exploration (Bohm, 1996; De Weerdt, 1999; Garvey et al., 2009; Gunnlaugson, 2007; Senge, 1990). Both parties suspend a need for closure and engage in dialogue for the purpose of expanding their understanding: for the coachee, understanding of themselves, and for the coach, understanding of the coachee.

OWNERSHIP

> **VIGNETTE**
>
> Just the breakthrough moment in understanding that it was my responsibility to take care of my own development.

The coach does not offer solutions, but instead emphasizes the need for the individual to take ownership for their own development. This is also a major theme of transformational learning, as discussed in Chapter 8. That this was a particularly profound discovery for the coachee is apparent from the vignette. Coaching provides the awareness of opportunities, and the realization that whatever objectives or outcomes the coachee may want to achieve will only become a reality if they take action in making it happen. However, the coaching process seems to give the permission and the nudge needed to realize that the choice of acting on ideas was their responsibility. A coach shared with me his thoughts on his own experiences and suggests that this was a light bulb moment for both him and a coachee who had hitherto perceived herself as a victim of circumstances that had kept her locked in to a reality that was both destructive and stifling to her wellbeing:

> **VIGNETTE**
>
> She realized she had the right to be who she wanted to be, she had a right to her life and the direction she wanted to go. She didn't have to wait for other people, she didn't have to wait for fate to play its hand, she didn't have to wait for circumstances to change, she had the right to take it and make her own mistakes.

It is worth reminding ourselves that the issue of ownership is one of the areas where power could be used and abused by either party. The need of the coachee to be given answers may mean that they manipulate the coach to provide them with solutions or objectives to pursue, thereby abdicating their personal power and ownership of the agenda. On the other hand, the coach may have a personal need to nurture or dominate the agenda and use their potential power to impose solutions on the coachee. As I have pointed out in Chapter 2, a potential weakness of a strong humanistic approach is a tendency to nurture and support, and for the coach to assume responsibility for the outcomes of the coaching intervention, thereby robbing the coachee of developing and pursuing her own choices.

The power of coaching is to release the coachee from an attitude or a belief that prevents them from realizing their potential and to create a reality that may be more enabling. William James (2000) is quoted to have said that 'The greatest discovery in our generation is that human beings, by changing the inner attitudes of their minds can change the outer aspects of their lives.' As Whitmore argues during an interview with Kauffman (2008), coaches do not bring wisdom; they evoke it in the coachee by drawing their own wisdom from them.

CONFIDENCE

The coaching experience also appears to generate a heightened sense of confidence within the coachee. In identifying the different phases of transformational learning, Mezirow (1981) includes the building of confidence. A lack of confidence in oneself can create barriers to achievement and opportunities for development. Higher confidence results in a higher sense of competence and therefore increased achievement. Developing greater confidence provides the individual with an increased ability to accept both their strengths as well as their perceived weaknesses. However, it is also true to say that the process of learning might also lead to frustration and a lack of confidence as the learner is exposed to new information and knowledge. The possible confidence and ownership developed through coaching provides the individual with the ability to change their worldview to be more enabling, as described by Mezirow and other transformative learning scholars in the previous chapter.

TRANSFORMATIVE LEARNING

Moore (2005) proposes that personal transformation is a journey that happens in stages. Mezirow (1991) recognizes that different people enter the transformational learning journey with different levels of readiness to transform their world-view. Change is seen as an unavoidable outcome of transformation, and that without change transformation does not occur. Mezirow (1991) concurs and suggests that this inner journey of transformation requires a helper (i.e., educator, teacher, coach, counsellor, facilitator, friend) who can support the individual in identifying and examining their assumptions that underlie beliefs, feelings and actions. What is important in this process is the non-judgemental approach of the coach or suspension of judgement as referred to by Bohm (1996). Suspension on the part of both parties allows for the exploration of assumptions, which eventually lead to trans-formative learning. Gunnlaugson (2007) suggests that suspension slows down the stream of consciousness, which allows the individual to reflect on it. This may be what is perceived as the sacred nature of the coaching space or bubble as a psychological space. Both coaches and coachees refer to the sense of time being suspended in this space.

One of the key assumptions associated with transformational learning is that it is rooted in the way people communicate, as put forward by Mezirow (1997). Gunnlaugson (2007) supports the assertion that transformation requires dialogue, and he suggests that it is communication which transcends discursive reason and facilitates meta-awareness within the learner. Drawing on the work of Bohm (1996), Gunnlaugson (2007: 139) puts forward a model of co-creative dialogue which supports my claims of the co-constructive nature of the coaching relationship. He defines a model of generative dialogue, which he perceives as a catalyst for transformational learning. It outlines the movement from 'conventional conversation (talking nice) to debate (talking tough) through to reflective enquiry (reflective dialogue) toward forms of co-creative engagement in the final field of generative dialogue'. He suggests that it is in the final field that the learner is able to explore in safety the assumptions they hold.

He concludes with the final stage, which he terms 'presencing', where the individual becomes aware of the possibilities of new knowledge unfolding.

Transformation is not necessarily one major event but may instead be a series of smaller events that collectively create transformation overall. However, it also seems that communicating and articulating the nature of values and beliefs is problematic when we try to express these through language, and is often associated with emotions. As we have seen, the change in worldview referred to by Mezirow (1991) and other proponents of transformational learning (Dirkx, 2001; Tennant, 2005) is accompanied by emotions. Dirkx (2001) states that emotion directs the learner's attention to the imaginative dimensions of their being, thereby connecting and integrating powerful feelings which often arise within the context of intellectual and cognitive development. Dirkx (2001: 132) also proposes that learning experiences that are meaningful are also deeply emotional, 'evoking powerful feelings, such as fear, grief, loss, regret, and anger, but also sometimes joy, wonder, and awe'.

For change to take place, one needs to understand why one does something in the first instance, and emotions are perceived as a route into the awareness that precedes change. There seems to be a general consensus that behaviours are the result of emotions and that emotions are in turn as a result of the values and beliefs that have been touched, much like a raw nerve. Through awareness and understanding of those emotions come the management of the response, leading, to a large extent, to an awareness of the available choices of response. The idea of choice and ownership is associated with transformational learning, and Cranton (1994) emphasizes the need for the learner to have ownership of the learning outcomes. This is reflected in the assumptions of coaching that the coachee owns and drives the agenda. It is seen as good and healthy to have emotions and emotional responses and that through awareness one is able to channel them in a positive way. This is an interesting area of research in psychology, namely positive psychology that advocates the need for the recognition, balance and in particular the inclusion of both negative and positive emotions. Emotions accompany the transition of assumptions, which ultimately lead to changes in behaviour.

THE SKILLED LEARNER

Much has been written about the skills of the coach, but very little is said about the skills of the coachee as an effective learner within the coaching process (Stokes, 2007). As very little is available by way of determining what involves being the skilled coachee, Stokes draws on the work of Pearn and Downs (1989), in which they list the attributes of the skilled learner in understanding what would be expected of a skilled coachee. The key message is that the skilled learner plays an active role in their own learning and that learning is gained through experience. This assumption is discussed at length in Chapter 2 and the literature on transformative learning is outlined in the previous chapter.

Learners are also expected to take responsibility for how they learn, and their learning is not necessarily seen as being dependent on the quality of the teaching. Questioning and feedback is perceived as important and to be sought by the student for the purpose of developing their performance. Skilled learners are also seen as being open to and seeking new learning opportunities. If philosophically the coach or facilitator of learning adopts the perspective outlined in this section, then the relationship becomes one of equals and shared partners in the journey of discovery. This also reinforces my argument made elsewhere that the inputs and outputs are not what drive the process, as it will be different from one coachee to another, depending on what they select as their learning experience. The selection of tools and techniques is therefore driven by the needs of the coachee and not the focus of the process.

In support of the concept of the skilled learner, a number of proponents of coaching suggest that the success of the coaching relationship is equally as dependent on the willingness of the coachee to be coached (Bachkirova, 2007; Fillery-Travis and Lane, 2007). I propose that the willingness to engage is a significant factor in a successful outcome. The coachee has to be prepared to enter into a deep and interpersonal communication with the coach (Quick and Macik-Frey, 2004), and as Hargrove (1995) suggests, it is through the coaching conversation that all coaching intervention takes place. It is true to say that the coaching relationship is like no other (Whitworth et al., 1998).

Whitworth et al. also suggest that its uniqueness is dependent on the state of the coach, namely that they strive to be without judgement and accepting the coachee exactly for what they are. Furthermore, the relationship is also influential in the quality of the coaching experience (Fillery-Travis and Lane, 2007; Mäthner et al., 2005; O'Broin and Palmer, 2007). However, it is a relationship that is transient by nature and it might be that this factor contributes to the quality of that relationship.

There is also a strong parallel between the role, characteristics and assumptions of the coach and that of the transformational teacher, as discussed in the review of the literature in Chapter 2. Trust is a key component that makes it possible to embark on the journey of inner learning facilitated by the coach. A contributing factor in establishing the sense of trust is associated with the independence of the coach from most aspects of the life of the coachee, both professionally and personally.

CO-CONSTRUCTION

A key factor I include in the black box of coaching is the co-constructive nature of coaching. Cox (2006) concurs and suggests that it allows the coachee to reflect on both knowledge and experience, past and present, for the purpose of generating new knowledge and understanding, which is identified as the process of transformation. As Mezirow (1990) and other transformative learning scholars propose, transformative learning does not happen in isolation and is indeed a social affair that requires interaction, debate and being exposed to the alternative realities presented by others. The literature on adult learning argues strongly that learning does not take place in isolation, but that it requires the interaction with others, in particular between the educator and learner. The same holds true for the insight the coachee gains as a result of the partnership with their coach. The principles of constructionism are evident as a condition of transformative learning and are discussed in Chapter 7.

Constructionism suggests that when people talk and engage with each other relationally, the world gets constructed. Burr (1995) suggests the term constructionism has taken shape against the backcloth of postmodernism and could therefore be defined as an ontology and theory of knowledge. However, from the literature on adult learning and the stories I have shared from both coaches as well as coachees throughout the book, I suggest it is also a practice for the purpose of constructing knowledge and understanding through the interaction with others; in the words of Weick (1995), to make sense of the world. Knowledge is not seen as having an independent existence, but instead is constructed through communal and participative relationships, such as that between the coach and coachee.

The elements of the coaching circle within the heuristic I created are interactive and the coachee may journey around the circle a number of times throughout the coaching experience. I furthermore suggest if the elements defined in the heuristic are present, coaching is more likely to lead to the transformation described throughout this book.

I have advocated in this book that the role of philosophy is significantly influential in the way the coach will approach their practice, and in the presence they will bring to the coaching space. Of equal importance is the role of philosophy in shaping and guiding the conversations about the future of coaching and all aspects associated with regulation of this emerging profession.

REFERENCES

Allan, J. G., Fairclough, G. and Frenzen, B. (2002) *The Power of the Tale: Using Narratives for Organisational Success.* Chichester: Wiley.

Alvesson, M. and Willmott, H. (1996) *Making Sense of Management: A Critical Introduction.* London: Sage.

Argyris, C. (1976) *Increasing Leadership Effectiveness.* New York: Wiley.

Argyris, M. and Schön, D. (1974) *Theory in Practice: Increasing Professional Effectiveness.* San Francisco: Jossey–Bass.

Askeland, M. K. (2009) 'A reflexive inquiry into the ideologies and theoretical assumptions of coaching', *Coaching, An International Journal of Theory, Research and Practice*, 2(1): 65–75.

Augustijnen, M-T., Schnitzer, G. and Van Esbroeck, R. (2011) 'A model of executive coaching: a qualitative study', *International Coaching Psychology Review*, 6(2): 150–64.

Bachkirova, T. (2007) 'Role of coaching psychology in defining boundaries between counseling and coaching', in S. Palmer and A. Whybrow (eds), *Handbook of Coaching Psychology: A Guide for Practitioners.* Hove: Routledge.

Bachkirova, T. and Kauffman, C. (2009) 'The blind men and the elephant: using criteria of universality and uniqueness in evaluating our attempts to define coaching', *Coaching: An International Journal of Theory, Research and Practice*, 2(2): 95–105.

Bak, P. (1997) *How Nature Works: The Science of Self-Organized Criticality.* London: Biddles.

Barker, R. and Gower, K. (2010) 'Strategic application of storytelling in organizations: toward effective communication in a diverse world', *Journal of Business Communication*, 47(3): 295–312.

Bateson, G. (1972) *Steps to An Ecology of Mind.* Chicago: University of Chicago Press.

Becker, G. (1997) *Disrupted Lives: How People Create Meaning in a Chaotic World.* Berkeley, CA: University of California Press.

Berger, P. and Luckmann, T. (1991) *The Social Construction of Reality: A Treatise in the Sociology of Knowledge.* London: Penguin Books.

Billett, S. (2004) 'Workplace participatory practices: conceptualising workplaces as learning environments', *Journal of Workplace Learning*, 16(6): 312–24.

Bluckert, P. (2005) 'The foundations of a psychological approach to executive coaching', *Industrial and Commercial Training*, 37(4): 171–8.

Bohm, D. (1996) *On Dialogue*, Lee Nichol (ed.), London: Routledge.

Boje, D. M. (1991) 'Consulting and change in the storytelling organization', *Journal of Organizational Change Management*, 4(3): 7–17.

Boje, D. M. (1995) 'Stories of the storytelling organization: a postmodern analysis of Disney as Tamara-Land', *Academy of Management Journal*, 38: 997–1035.

Boje, D. M. (2008) *Storytelling Organizations*. London: Sage.

Boje, D. M., Luhmann, J. T. and Baack, D. E. (1999) 'Hegemonic stories and encounters between storytelling organizations', *Journal of Management Inquiry*, 8(4): 340–60.

Boland, Jr R. J. (1984) 'Sense-making of accounting data as a technique of organizational diagnosis', *Management Science*, 30(7): 868–82.

Boudens, C. J. (2005) 'The story of work: a narrative analysis of workplace emotion', *Organization Studies*, 26(9): 1285–306.

Bradbury, H., Mirvis, P., Neilsen, E. and Pasmore, W. (2008) 'Action research at work: creating the future following the path from Lewin', in P. Reason and H. Bradbury (eds), *The SAGE Handbook of Action Research: Participative Inquiry and Practice*, 2nd edn. London: Sage.

Brendel, W. (2009) 'A Framework for Narrative-Driven Transformative Learning in Medicine', *Journal of Transformative Education*, 7(1): 26–43.

Brockbank, A. and McGill, I. (1998) *Facilitating Reflective Learning in Higher Education* (2nd edn). Berkshire: Open University Press, McGraw-Hill Education.

Brockbank, A. and McGill, I. (2006) *Facilitating Reflective Learning in Higher Education*. Buckingham: Sage and Open University Press.

Brookfield, S. (1995) 'Adult learning: an overview', in A. Tuijnman (ed.), *International Encyclopaedia of Education*. Oxford: Pergamon Press.

Brown, A. D., Yiannis, G. and Gherardi, S. (2009) 'Storytelling and change: an unfolding story', *Organization*, 16(3): 323–33.

Brown, R. H. (1994) 'Reconstructing social theory after the postmodern critique', in H. W. Simons and M. Billig, *After Postmodernism: Reconstructing Ideology Critique*. London: Sage.

Bruner, J. (1986) *Actual Minds, Impossible Worlds*. Cambridge, MA: Harvard University Press.

Bruner, J. (1990) *Acts of Meaning*. Cambridge, MA: Harvard University Press.

Bruner, J. (1991) 'The narrative construction of reality', *Critical Inquiry*, 18 (Autumn): 1–21.

Bruner, J. (2002) *Making Stories: Law, Literature, Life*. Cambridge, MA: Harvard University Press.

Brunning, H. (2006) *Executive Coaching: Systems Psychodynamic Perspective*, London: Karnac Books.

Burkitt, I. (1999) 'Relational moves and generative dances', in S. McNamee and K. J. Gergen (eds), *Relational Responsibility: Resources for Sustainable Dialogue*. Thousand Oaks, CA: Sage.

Burr, V. (1995) *An Introduction to Social Constructionism*. London: Routledge.

Burrell, G. and Morgan, G. (1979) *Sociological Paradigms and Organisational Analysis*. London: Heinemann Educational Books Ltd.

Campbell, D. (2000) *The Socially Constructed Organization*. London: H. Karnac (Books).

Carr, A. N. and Ann, C. (2011) 'Introduction. The use and abuse of storytelling in organizations', *Journal of Management Development*, 30(2): 236–46.

Cavanagh, M. and Lane, D. (2012) 'Coaching psychology coming of age: the challenges we face in the messy world of complexity', *International Coaching Psychology Review*, 7(1): 75–90.

Chapman, T., Best, B. and Van Casteren, P. (2003) *Executive Coaching: Exploding the Myths*. Basingstoke: Palgrave Macmillan.

Cilliers, P. (1998) *Complexity and Postmodernism: Understanding Complex Systems*. London: Routledge.

Clutterbuck, D. and Lane, G. (2004) *The Situational Mentor: An International Review of Competences and Capabilities in Mentoring*. Aldershot: Gower.

Clutterbuck, D. and Megginson, D. (2005) *Making Coaching Work: Creating a Coaching Culture*. London: The Chartered Institute of Personnel and Development (CIPD).

Clutterbuck, D. and Megginson, D. (2011) 'Coach maturity: an emerging concept', in L. Wildflower and D. Brennan (eds), *The Theory and Practice of Evidence-Based Coaching*. Hoboken, NJ: Wiley.

Colville, I. D., Waterman, R. H. and Weick, K. E. (1999) 'Organizing and the search for excellence: making sense of the times in theory and practice', *Organization*, 6(1): 129–48.

Conant R. C. and Ashby, R. W. (1970) 'Every good regulator of a system must be a good model of that system', *International Journal of Systems Assignments*, 1(2): 89–97.

Conle, C. (2000) 'Thesis as Narrative or "What is the Inquiry in Narrative Inquiry?"', *Curriculum Inquiry*, 30(2): 189–214

Cope, M. (2004) *The Seven Cs of Coaching: The Definitive Guide to Collaborative Coaching*. Harlow: Pearson Education Ltd.

Cox, E. (2006) 'An adult learning approach to coaching', in D. R. Stober and A. M. Grant (eds), *Evidence Based Coaching Handbook*. Hoboken, NJ: Wiley.

Cox, E. (2010) 'Last things first: ending well in the coaching relationship', in S. Palmer and A. McDowall (eds), *The Coaching Relationship: Putting People First*. London: Routledge.

Cox, E., Bachkirova, T. and Clutterbuck, D. (eds) (2010) *The Complete Handbook of Coaching*. London: Sage.

Cranton, P. (1994) *Understanding and Promoting Transformative Learning: A Guide for Educators of Adults*. San Francisco, CA: Jossey–Bass.

Cranton, P. (1996) *Professional Development as Transformative Learning: New Perspectives for Teachers of Adults.* San Francisco, CA: Jossey–Bass.

Cranton, P. (ed.) (1997) *Tranformative Learning in Action: Insights from Practice.* San Francisco, CA: Jossey–Bass.

Csikszentmihalyi, M. (2002) *Flow.* London: Rider.

Cummings, S. (2002) *ReCreating Strategy.* London: Sage.

Czarniawska, B. (1997) *Narrating the Organization: Dramas of Institutional Identity.* Chicago, IL: University of Chicago Press.

Day, C. and Leitch, R. (2001) 'Teachers' and teacher educators' lives: the role of emotion', *Teacher and Teaching Education*, 17: 403–15.

De Haan, E. (2008) *Relational Coaching: Journeys towards Mastering One-to-One Learning.* Chichester: Wiley.

De Haan, E. (2011) 'Back to basics: how the discovery of transference is relevant for coaches and consultants today', *International Coaching Psychology Review*, 6(2): 180–93.

De Haan, E. (2012) 'Back to basics II: How the research on attachment and reflective-self function is relevant for coaches and consultants today', *International Coaching Psychology Review*, 7(2): 194–209.

De Haan, E. and Burger, Y. (2005) *Coaching with Colleagues: An Action Guide for One-to-One Learning.* Basingstoke: Palgrave Macmillan.

Denzin, N. K. and Lincoln, Y. (eds) (2000) *Handbook of Qualitative Research*, 2nd edn. Thousand Oaks, CA: Sage.

De Vries, M. F. R. K. (1989) 'Leaders who self-destruct: the causes and cures', *Organizational Dynamics*, 17: 5–17.

De Vries, M. F. R. K., Korotov, K. and Florent-Treacy, E. (2007) *Coach and Couch: The Psychology of Making Better Leaders.* Basingstoke: Palgrave Macmillan.

De Weerdt, S. (1999) 'Dialoging: exploring the dialectics', *Emergence*, 1(3): 64–70.

Dewey, J. (1938) *Experience and Education.* New York: Collier Books.

Dirkx, J. M. (2001) 'The power of feelings: emotion, imagination, and the construction of meaning in adult learning', *New Directions for Adult And Continuing Education*, 89, Spring: 63–72.

Dixon, N. M. (1999) *The Organizational Learning Cycle: How We Can Learn Collectively*, 2nd edn. London: Gower.

Dobson, K. S. and Block, L. (1988) 'Historical and philosophical bases of the cognitive-behavioural therapies', in K. S. Dobson (ed.), *Handbook of Cognitive-Behavioural Therapies*, 2nd edn. New York: Guilford Press.

Dobson, K. S. and Dozois, D. J. (2001) 'Historical and philosophical bases of the cognitive-behavioural therapies', in K. S. Dobson (ed.), *Handbook of Cognitive-Behavioural Therapies*, 2nd edn. New York: Guilford Press.

Dougherty, D., Borrelli, L., Munir, K. and O'Sullivan, A. (2000) 'Systems of organizational sensemaking for sustained product innovation', *Journal of Engineering and Technology Management*, 17: 321–55.

Downey, M. (2003) *Effective Coaching: Lessons from the Coach's Coach*, 2nd edn. New York: Texere.

Drake, D. B. (2007) 'The art of thinking narratively: implications for coaching psychology and practice', *Australian Psychologist*, 42(4): 283–94.

Drake, B. D. (2011) 'What do coaches need to know? Using the Mastery Window to assess and develop expertise', *Coaching: An International Journal of Theory, Research and Practice*, 4(2): 138–55.

Ducharme, M. J. (2004) 'The cognitive-behavioral approach to executive coaching', *Consulting Psychology Journal: Practice and Research*, 56(4): 214–24.

Du Toit, A. (2007) 'Making sense through coaching', *Journal of Management Development*, 26 (3): 281–291.

Du Toit, A. (2010) 'A hermeneutic study investigation of the relationship between coaching and adult learning'. PhD thesis, Sheffield–Hallam University.

Du Toit, A. and Reissner, S. (2010) 'Power and the tale: coaching as storyselling', *Journal of Management Development*, 30(3): 247–59.

Du Toit, A. and Sim, S. (2010) *Rethinking Coaching: Critical Theory and Economic Crisis*. London: Palgrave.

Easterby-Smith, M., Thorpe, R. and Lowe, A. (1991) *Management Research: An Introduction*, London: Sage.

Eden, C. and Ackermann, F. (1998) *Making Strategy: The Journey of Strategic Management*. London: Sage.

Edmonds, D. and Eidinow, J. (2001) *Wittgenstein's Poker: The Story of a Ten-Minute Argument between Two Great Philosophers*. New York: Harper Collins.

Ellinor, L. and Gerard, G. (1998) *Dialogue: Rediscover the Transforming Power of Conversation*. New York: Wiley.

Feyerabend, P. (1987) *Farewell to Reason*. London: Verso.

Fillery-Travis, A. and Lane, D. (2007) 'Research: Does coaching work?', in S. Palmer and A. Whybrow (eds), *Handbook of Coaching Psychology: A Guide for Practitioners*. Hove: Routledge.

Foucault, M. (2006) *The History of Madness*. Oxford: Routledge.

Fry, H., Ketteridge, S. and Marshall, S. (1999) *A Handbook for Teaching and Learning in Higher Education: Enhancing Academic Practice*. London: Kogan Page.

Gabriel, Y. (1991) 'On organizational stories and myths: why it is easier to slay a dragon than to kill a myth', *International Sociology*, 6(4): 427–42.

Gabriel, Y. (2000) *Storytelling in Organizations: Fact, Fictions and Fantasies*. Oxford: Oxford University Press.

Gabriel, Y. (2004) *Myths, Stories and Organizations*. Oxford: Oxford University Press.

Gallwey, T. (1974) *The Inner Game of Tennis: The Classic Guide to the Mental Side of Peak Performance*. New York: Random House.

Garvey, R. (2011) *A Very Short, Fairly Interesting and Reasonably Cheap Book about Coaching and Mentoring*. London: Sage.

Garvey, R., Stokes, P. and Megginson, D. (2009) *Coaching and Mentoring: Theory and Practice*. London: Sage.

Gergen, K. J. (1985) 'The social constructionist movement in modern psychology', *American Psychologist*, 40(3): 266–75.

Gergen, K. J. (1991) *The Saturated Self: Dilemmas of Identity in Contemporary Life*. New York: Basic Books.

Gergen, K. J. (1994) *Toward Transformation in Social Knowledge*, 2nd edn. London: Sage.

Gergen, K. J. (1997) *Realities and Relationships: Soundings in Social Construction*. Cambridge, MA: Harvard University Press.

Gergen, K. J. (1999) *An Invitation to Social Construction*. London: Sage.

Gergen, K. J. (2001) *Social Construction in Context*. London: Sage.

Gergen, K. J. and Gergen, M. M. (2008) 'Social construction and research as action', in P. Reason and H. Bradbury (eds), *The SAGE Handbook of Action Research: Participative Inquiry and Practice*, 2nd edn. London: Sage.

Gibb, S. (2008) *Human Resource Development: Process, Practices and Perspectives*, 2nd edn. Basingstoke: Palgrave Macmillan.

Gibb, S. and Hill, P. (2006) 'From trail-blazing individualism to a social construction community: modeling knowledge construction in coaching', *International Journal of Mentoring and Coaching*, IV(2): 58–77.

Giglio, T. D. and Urban, J. M. (1998) 'Coaching a leader: leveraging change at the top', *Journal of Management Development*, 17(2): 93–105.

Gioia, D. A. (2006) 'On Weick: an appreciation', *Organization Studies*, 27(11): 1709–21.

Grady, D. (2001) 'Work-based learning, action learning and the virtual paradigm', *Journal of Further and Higher Education*, 25(3): 315–24.

Grant, A. M. (2007) 'Past, present and future: the evolution of professional coaching and coaching psychology', in S. Palmer and A. Whybrow (eds), *Handbook of Coaching Psychology: A Guide for Practitioners*. Hove: Routledge.

Grant, A. M. (2012) 'ROS is a poor measure of coaching success: towards a more holistic approach using a well-being and engagement framework', *Coaching: An International Journal of Theory: Research and Practice*, 5(2): 74–85.

Grant, A. M. and Palmer, S. (2002) Coaching psychology. Meeting held at the annual conference of the Division of Counselling Psychology, British Psychological Society, Torquay, 18 May.

Gray, D. (2001) 'Work-based Learning, Action Learning and the Virtual Paradigm', *Journal of Further and Higher Education*, 25(3): 315–324.

Gray, D. E. (2006) 'Executive coaching: towards a dynamic alliance of psychotherapy and transformational learning processes', *Management Learning*, 37(4): 475–97.

Greenberg, L. S. and Bolger, E. (2001) 'An emotion-focused approach to the regulation of emotion and emotional pain', *Journal of Clinical Psychology*, 57: 197–211.

Grisham, T. (2006) 'Metaphor, poetry, storytelling and cross-cultural leadership', *Management Decision*, 44(4): 486–503.

Gunnlaugson, O. (2007) 'Shedding light on the underlying forms of transformative learning theory: introducing three distinct categories of consciousness', *Journal of Transformative Education*, 5(2): 134–51.

Habermas, J. (1971) *Knowledge and Human Interests*. Boston, MA: Beacon Press.

Hansen, C. and Kahnweiler, W. (1993) 'Storytelling, an instrument for understanding organizational dynamics', *Human Relations*, 6(12): 1391–1409.

Hargrove, R. (1995) *Masterful Coaching*. San Francisco, CA: Jossey–Bass Pfeiffer.

Harrison, R. (2005) *Learning and Development*, 4th edn. London: CIPD.

Hart, V., Blattner, J. and Leipsic, S. (2001) 'Coaching versus therapy: A perspective', *Consulting Psychology Journal: Practice and Research*, 53(4): 229–37.

Hassard, J. (1994) 'Postmodern organizational analysis: Toward a conceptual framework', *Journal of Management Studies*, 31(3): 303–24.

Hodge, B. (2012) 'The challenges we face in the messy world of complexity: a response', *International Coaching Psychology Review*, 7(1): 109–13.

Holman, D., Pavlica, K. and Thorpe, R. (1997) 'Rethinking Kolb's theory of experiential learning in management education', *Management Learning*, 28(2): 135–48.

Horrocks, A. and Callahan, J. L. (2006) 'The role of emotion and narrative in the reciprocal construction of identity', *Human Resource Development International*, 9(1): 69–83.

Hume, D. (1962) *A Treatise of Human Nature* (ed. D. G. C. Macnabb). Glasgow: William Collins.

Huzzard, T. (2004) 'Communities of domination? Reconceptualising organisational learning and power', *Journal of Workplace Learning*, 16(6): 250–361.

Hyater-Adams, Y. A. (2011) 'Learning diversity and leadership skills through transformative narratives', *Tamara Journal for Critical Organization Inquiry*, 8(4): 208–32.

Illeris, K. (2004) 'A model for learning in working life', *Journal of Workplace Learning*, 16(8): 431–41.

James, C. H. and Minnis, W. C. (2004) 'Organizational storytelling: it makes sense', *Business Horizons*, 47(4): 23–32.

James, W. (2000) *Pragmatism and Other Writings*. USA: Penguin Group US.

Janis, Irving L. (1972) *Victims of Groupthink*. Boston, MA: Houghton Mifflin.

Janis, Irving L. (1982) *Groupthink: Psychological Studies of Policy Decisions and Fiascoes*, 2nd edn. Boston, MA: Houghton Mifflin.

Jones, G. and Spooner, K. (2006) 'Coaching high achievers', *Consulting Psychology Journal: Practice and Research*, 58(1): 40–50.

Jones, R. S. P. (2012) 'Coaching psychology and research evidence: the role of scepticism', *The Coaching Psychologist*, 8(2): 93–5.

Joseph, S. and Bryant-Jefferies, R. (2007) 'Person-centred coaching psychology', in S. Palmer and A. Whybrow (eds), *Handbook of Coaching Psychology: A Guide for Practitioners*. Hove: Routledge.

Joy-Matthews, J., Megginson, D. and Surtees, M. (2004) *Human Resource Development*. London: Kogan Page.

Kadembo, E. M. (2012) 'Anchored in the story: the core of human understanding, branding, education, socialisation and the shaping of values', *The Marketing Review*, 12(3): 221–31.

Kahn, M. S. (2011) 'Coaching on the axis: an integrative and systemic approach to business coaching', *International Coaching Psychology Review*, 6(2): 194–210.

Kampa-Kokesch, S. and Anderson, M. Z. (2001) 'Executive coaching: a comprehensive review of the literature', *Consulting Psychology Journal: Practice and Research*, 53(4): 205–28.

Kauffman, C. (2008) 'The evolution of coaching: an interview with Sir John Whitmore', *Coaching: An International Journal of Theory, Research and Practice*, 1(1): 11–15.

Kauffman, S. (1995) *At Home in the Universe*. Oxford: Oxford University Press.

Kelly, G. A. (1955) *The Psychology of Personal Constructs*. New York: Norton.

Kelly, G. A. (1991) *The Psychology of Personal Constructs, Volume Two: Clinical Diagnosis and Psychotherapy*. London: Routledge.

Kemp, T. J. (2008) 'Searching for the elusive model of coaching: could the "Holy Grail" be right in front of us?', *International Psychology Review*, 3(3): 219–26.

Kerby, A. P. (1991) *Narrative and the Self*. Indianapolis, IN: Indiana University Press.

Kilburg, R. R. (2002) 'Failure and Negative Outcomes: The taboo topic in Executive Coaching', in C. Fitzgerald & J. Garvey Berger (eds) *Executive Coaching: Practices and Perspectives*. Palo Alto, CA: Davies-Black Publishing, 283–301.

Knowles, M. (1980) *The modern practice of adult education: from pedagogy to andragogy*. Englewood Cliffs, NJ: Prentice Hall/Cambridge University Press.

Lämsä, A-M. and Sintonen, T. (2006) 'A narrative approach for organizational learning in a diverse organisation', *Journal of Workplace Learning*, 18(2): 106–20.

Land, K. (2007) 'Storytelling as therapy: the motives of a counselor', *Business Communication Quarterly*, September: 377–82.

Lapp, C. A. and Carr, A. N. (2008) 'Coaching can be storyselling: creating change through crises of confidence', *Journal of Organizational Change Management*, 21(5): 532–59.

Lenhardt, V. (2004) *Coaching for Meaning*. Basingstoke: Palgrave Macmillan.

Lewin, R. (1993) *Complexity: Life at the Edge of Chaos*, New York: Macmillan.

Linde, C. (1993) *Life Stories: The Creation of Coherence*. New York: Oxford University Press.

Linley, P. A. and Harrington, S. (2007) 'Integrating positive psychology and coaching psychology: shared assumptions and aspirations?', in S. Palmer and A. Whybrow (eds), *Handbook of Coaching Psychology: A Guide for Practitioners*. Hove: Routledge.

Linstead, S. (1994) 'Objectivity, reflexivity and fiction: humanity, inhumanity and the science of the social', *Human Relations*, 47: 1321–1346.

Linstead, S. (2004) 'Deconstruction in the study of organizations', in J. Hassard and M. Parker (eds), *Postmodernism and Organizations*. London: Sage.

Lizzio, A. and Wilson, K. (2004) 'Action learning in higher education: an investigation of its potential to develop professional capability', *Studies in Higher Education*, 29(4): 469–88.

Luebbe, D. M. (2005) 'The three-way mirror of executive coaching', *Dissertation Abstracts International: Section B (The Sciences & Engineering)*, 66: 1771.

Luhman, J. T and Boje, D. M. (2001) 'What is Complexity Science? A Possible Answer from Narrative Research', *Emergence*, 3(1): 158–168.

Lyotard, J-F. (1979) *The Postmodern Condition: A Report on Knowledge* (trans. G. Bennington and B. Massumi). Manchester: Manchester University Press.

Marion, R. (1999) *The Edge of Organization: Chaos and Complexity Theories of Formal Social Systems*. Thousand Oaks, CA: Sage.

Mäthner, D E., Jansen, A. and Bachmann T. (2005) 'Wirsamkeit und Wirkung von Coaching', in C. Rauen (ed.), *Handbuch Coaching*, 3rd edn. Goettingen: Hogrefe.

McAdams, D. P. (1997) *The Stories We Live By: Personal Myths and the Making of the Self.* New York: Guilford Press.

McAuley, J., Duberley, J. and Johnson, P. (2006) *Organization Theory: Challenges and Perspectives*. Hemel Hempstead: Financial Times Prentice Hall.

McComb, C. (2012) 'Developing coaching culture: are your coaching relationships healthy?', *Industrial and Commercial Training*, 44(4): 232–5.

McNamee, S. K. J. and Gergen, K. J. (1999) *Relational Responsibility: Resources for Sustainable Dialogue*. Thousand Oaks, CA: Sage.

Mezirow, J. (1981) 'A critical theory of adult learning and education', *Adult Education Quarterly*, 32: 3–24.

Mezirow, J. (1990) 'How critical reflection triggers transformative learning', in J. Mezirow (ed.), *Fostering Critical Reflection in Adulthood: A Guide to Transformative and Emancipatory Learning*. San Francisco, CA: Jossey–Bass.

Mezirow, J. (1991) *Transformative Dimensions of Adult Learning*, San Francisco, CA: Jossey–Bass.

Mezirow, J. (1994) 'Understanding transformation theory', *Adult Education Quarterly*, 44(4): 222–3.

Mezirow, J. (1996) 'Contemporary Paradigms of Learning', *Education Quarterly*, 46(3): 158–73.

Mezirow, J. (1997) 'Transformative learning: theory to practice', in P. Cranton (ed.), *Transformative Learning in Action: Insights froms Practice*. San Francisco, CA: Jossey–Bass.

Moen, F. and Federici, R. A. (2012) 'The effect from external executive coaching', *Coaching: An International Journal of Theory, Research and Practice*, 5(2): 113–31.

Moon, J. A. (2006) *Learning Journals: A Handbook for Reflective Practice and Professional Development*, 2nd edn. London: Routledge.

Moore, J. (2005) 'Is Higher Education Ready for Transformative Learning?: A Question Explored in the Study of Sustainability', *Journal of Transformative Education*, 3(1): 76–91.

Morgan, G. (1983) *Beyond Method: Strategies for Social Research*. Thousand Oaks, CA: Sage.

Morgan, G. (1997) *Images of Organization*. Thousand Oaks, CA: Sage.

Morgan, G. and Smircich, L. (1980) 'The case for qualitative research', *Academy of Management Review*, 5(4): 491–500.

Mumby, D. K. and Clair, R. (1997) 'Organizational discourse', in van Dijk, T. A. (ed.) *Discourse as Structure and Process: Discourse Studies Volume 2*, London: Sage.

Neale, S., Spencer-Arnell, L. and Wilson, L. (2009) *Emotional Intelligence Coaching: Improving Performance for Leaders, Coaches and the Individual*. London: Kogan Page.

Nelson, E. and Hogan, R. (2009) 'Coaching on the dark side', *International Coaching Psychology Review*, 4(1): 9–21.

Nonaka, I. and Takeuchi, H. (1995) *The Knowledge-Creating Company*. Oxford: Oxford University Press.

O'Broin, A. and Palmer, S. (2007) 'Reappraising the coach–client relationship: the unassuming change agent in coaching', in S. Palmer and A. Whybrow (eds), *Handbook of Coaching Psychology: A Guide for Practitioners*. Hove: Routledge.

O'Donoghue, J. and Maguire, T. (2005) 'The individual learner, employability and the workplace: a reappraisal of relationships and prophecies', *Journal of European Industrial Training*, 29(6): 436–46.

O'Neill, M. B. (2000) *Executive Coaching with Backbone and Heart: A Systems Approach to Engaging Leaders with their Challenges*. San Francisco, CA: Jossey–Bass.

Palmer, S. and Szymanska, K. (2007) 'Cognitive behavioural coaching: an integrative approach', in S. Palmer and A. Whybrow (eds), *Handbook of Coaching Psychology: A Guide for Practitioners*. Hove: Routledge.

Palmer S. and Whybrow A. (eds) (2007) *Handbook of Coaching Psychology: A Guide for Practitioners*. Hove: Routledge.

Parker, T. S. (2006) 'Changing emotion: the use of therapeutic storytelling', *Journal of Marital and Family Therapy*, 32(2): 155–66.

Pascale, R. T., Millemann, M. and Gioja, L. (2000) *Surfing the Edge of Chaos*. New York: Crown Publishers.

Passmore, J. (2007) 'Behavioural coaching', in S. Palmer and A. Whybrow (eds), *Handbook of Coaching Psychology: A Guide for Practitioners*. Hove: Routledge.

Passmore, J. and McGoldrick, S. (2009) 'Super-vision, extra-vision or blind faith? A grounded theory study of the efficacy of coaching supervision', *International Coaching Psychology Review*, 4(2): 145–61.

Pearn, M. and Downs, S. (1989) 'Developing skilled learners: a strategy for coping with new technology', *Industrial and Commercial Training*, 21: 9–17.

Pedler, M. and Burgoyne, J. (2008) 'Action learning', in P. Reason and H. Bradbury (eds), *The Sage Handbook of Action Research: Participative Inquiry and Practice*, 2nd edn. London: Sage.

Peltier, B. (2009) *The Psychology of Executive Coaching: Theory and Application*, 2nd edn. London: Routledge.

Peterson, D. B. (2006) 'People are complex and the world is messy: a behavior-based approach to executive coaching', in D. R. Stober and A. M. Grant (eds), *Evidence Based Coaching Handbook*. Hoboken, NJ: Wiley.

Pounder, J. S. (2006) 'Transformational classroom leadership', *Educational Management Administration and Leadership*, 34(4): 533–45.

Pratt, M. G. (2000) 'The good, the bad, and the ambivalent: managing identification among Amway distributors', *Administrative Science Quarterly*, 25(3): 456–93.

Price, J. (2009) 'The coaching/therapy boundary in organizational coaching', *Coaching: An International Journal of Theory, Research and Practice*, 2(2): 135–48.

Quick, J. C. and Macik-Frey, M. (2004) 'Behind the mask: coaching through deep interpersonal communication', *Consulting Psychology Journal: Practice and Research*, Spring, 56(2): 67–74.

Reason, P. and Bradbury, H. (eds) (2008) *The Sage Handbook of Action Research: Participative Inquiry and Practice*, 2nd edn. London: Sage.

Reissner, S. and du Toit, A. (2011) 'Power and the tale: storyselling', *Journal of Management Development*, 30(3): 247–59.

Riessman, C. K. (1993) *Narrative Analysis*. Newbury Park, CA: Sage.

Robotham, D. (2004) 'Developing the competent learner', *Industrial & Commercial Training*, 36(20): 66–72.

Rogers, C. R. (1967) *On Becoming a Person*. London: Constable.

Rogers, C. R. (1980) *A Way of Being*. New York: Mariner Books.

Sadler-Smith, E. (2006) *Learning and Development for Managers: Perspectives from Research and Practice*. Oxford: Blackwell.

Senge, P. (1990) *The Fifth Discipline: The Art and Practice of the Learning Organization*. London: Routledge.

Sherrill, J. A. (1999) 'Preparing teachers for leadership roles in the 21st century', *Theory into Practice*, 38(1): 533–45.

Shotter, J. (1993) *Conversational Realities: Constructing Life through Language*. London: Sage Publications.

Silsbee, D. (2008) *Presence-Based Coaching: Cultivating Self-Generative Leaders Through Mind, Body and Heart*. San Francisco, CA: Jossey–Bass.

Sim, S. (2001) *Gadamer*. London: Routledge.

Sim, S. (2004) *Fundamentalist World: The New Dark Age of Dogma*. Cambridge: Icon Press.

Skiffington, S. and Zeus, P. (2003) *Behavioural Coaching: How to Build Sustainable Personal and Organizational Strength*. Sydney: McGraw–Hill Australia.

Small, M. W. (2003) 'Philosophy in management: a new trend in management development', *Philosophy in Management*, 23(2): 183–96.

Smircich, L. and Stubbart, C. (1985) 'Strategic management in an enacted world', *Academy of Management Review*, 10(4): 724–36.

Sparrowe, R. T. (2005) 'Authentic Leadership and the Narrative Self', *The Leadership Quarterly*, 16: 419–39.

Spinelli, E. (2008) 'Coaching and therapy: similarities and divergences', *International Psychology Review*, 3(3): 219–26.

Stacey, R. D. (1996) *Complexity and Creativity in Organizations*. San Francisco, CA: Berrett–Koehler.

Stacey, R. D. (2000) *Strategic Management and Organisational Dynamics*, 3rd edn. Harlow: Pearson Education.

Stacey, R. (2012) 'Comment on debate article: Coaching psychology coming of age: the challenges we face in the messy world of complexity', *International Coaching Psychology Review*, 7(1): 91–5.

Steier, F. (1991) *Research and Reflexivity*. London: Sage.

Stein, I. F. (2009) 'Which hat am I wearing now? An evidence-based tool for coaching self-reflection', *Coaching: An International Journal of Theory, Research and Practice*, 2(2): 163–75.

Stern, D. N. (2004) *The Present Moment in Psychotherapy and Everyday Life*. New York: W. W. Norton.

Stewart, L. J., O'Riordan, S. and Palmer, S. (2008) 'Before we know how we've done, we need to know what we're doing: operationalising coaching to provide a foundation for coaching evaluation', *The Coaching Psychologist*, 4(3): 127–33.

Stober, D. R. (2006) 'Coaching from the humanistic perspective', in D. R. Stober and A. M. Grant (eds), *Evidence Based Coaching Handbook*. Hoboken, NJ: Wiley.

Stober, D. R. (2008) 'Making it stick: coaching as a tool for organizational change', *Coaching: An International Journal of Theory, Research and Practice*, 1(1): 71–80.

Stokes, P. (2007) The Skilled Coachee. EMCC European Conference, Stockholm.

Strauss, K., Griffin, M. A. and Rafferty, A. E. (2008) 'Proactivity directed toward the team and organization: the role of leadership, commitment and role-breadth self-efficacy, *British Journal of Management*, 20: 279–91.

Taylor, S. S. (1999) 'Making sense of revolutionary change: differences in members' stories', *Journal of Organizational Change Management*, 12(6): 524–39.

Taylor, S. S., Fisher, D. and Dufresne, R. L. (2004) 'The aesthetics of management storytelling: a key to organizational learning', in C. Grey and E. Antonacopoulou (eds), *Essential Readings in Management Learning*. London: Sage.

Tennant, M. (2005) 'Transforming Selves', *Journal of Transformative Education*, 3(2): 102–15.

Varela, F. J., Thompson, E. and Rosch, E. (1991) *The Embodied Mind: Cognitive Science and Human Experience*. Cambridge, MA: MIT Press.

von Glasersfeld, E. (1984) 'An introduction to radical constructivism', in P. Watzlawick (ed.), *The Invented Reality*. New York: W. W. Norton.

Voronov, M. (2008) 'Toward engaged critical management studies', *Organization*, 15(6): 939–45.

Vygotsky, L. S. (1978) *Mind and Society: The Development of Higher Mental Processes*. Cambridge, MA: Harvard University Press.

Waldrop, M. M. (1992) *Complexity: The Emerging Science at the Edge of Order and Chaos*. New York: Simon & Schuster.

Wasylyshyn, K. M. (2003) 'Executive coaching: an outcome study', *Consulting Psychology Journal: Practice and Research*, 55(2): 94–106.

Weick, K. E. (1979) *The Social Psychology of Organizing*, 2nd edn. New York: McGraw-Hill.

Weick, K. E. (1995) *Sensemaking in Organizations*. Thousand Oaks, CA: Sage.

Weick, K. E. and Browning, L. D. (1986) 'Argument and narration in organizational communication', *Journal of Management*, 12: 243–59.

Weick, K. E., Sutcliffe, K. M. and Obstfeld, D. (2005) 'Organizing and the process of sensemaking', *Organization Science*, 16(4): 409–21.

Weiner, B. (1985) 'An attributional theory of achievement motivation and emotion', *Psychological Review*, 92: 548–73.

Welman, P. and Bachkirova, T. (2010) 'The issue of power in the coaching relationship', in S. Palmer and A. McDowall (eds), *The Coaching Relationship*. London: Routledge.

Werner, J. M. and DeSimone, R. L. (2005) *Human Resource Development*, 4th edn. Mason, OH: South Western Educational.

Whitmore, J. (1996) *Coaching for Performance: Growing People, Performance and Purpose*, 2nd edn. London: Nicholas Brealey.

Whitmore, J. (2011) 'Coaching in the recession', *Coaching: An International Journal of Theory, Research and Practice*, 4(1): 50–4.

Whitworth, L., Kimsey-House, H. and Sandahl, P. (1998) *Co-Active Coaching: New Skills for Coaching People Toward Success in Work and Life*. Palo Alto, CA: Davies–Black.

Whybrow, A. (2008) 'Coaching psychology: coming of age?' *International Psychology Review*, 3(3): 219–26.

Whybrow, A., Grant, A. M., Palmer, S. and Kemp, T. (2012) 'Editorial: Coaching psychology coming of age', *International Coaching Psychology Review*, 7(1): 72–4.

Wilson, C. (2007) *Best Practice in Performance Coaching: A Handbook for Leaders, Coaches, HR Professionals and Organizations*. London: Kogan Page.

Witherspoon, R. and White, R. P. (1996) 'Executive coaching: What's in it for you?', *Training and Development Journal*, 50: 14–15.

Winch, A. and Ingram, H. (2004) 'Activating learning through the lifetime navigator: a tool for reflection', *International Journal of Contemporary Hospitality Management*, 16(4): 231–6.

Wittgenstein, L. (2001) *Philosophical Investigations*. Anscombe, G. E. M. (Trans). Oxford: Blackwell Publishers Ltd.

INDEX